T0209211

Love Letters in the Sand

Ayla's Faith

Bella Louise Allen

authorHOUSE®

AuthorHouse™
1663 Liberty Drive
Bloomington, IN 47403
www.authorhouse.com
Phone: 1 (800) 839-8640

Published by AuthorHouse 08/26/2016

ISBN: 978-1-5246-2521-4 (sc)
ISBN: 978-1-5246-2519-1 (hc)
ISBN: 978-1-5246-2520-7 (e)

Library of Congress Control Number: 2016913546

Print information available on the last page.

Dear readers: LOVE LETTERS IN THE SAND- AYLA'S FAITH is a love affair that started many years ago.

Not just my own love affair. It is a love affair just like your own. I desire to love and to do well. We all start out this way. Somewhere along the way we tend to lose the flame. The desire if you will.

Some of us have an easier time holding onto this love. His love. Some of us lose His love very early on and struggle to find it again.

This love story is my personal journey with God, my master teachers, high ranking angels, earth angels that I knew and loved and my love for nature and all that God has to offer each of us.

My story that I present to those who are willing to open their hearts and let God's love shine in will witness communication between a beautiful angel taken from us way too soon.

To protect this earth angel and her loving family that she tries desperately to connect with from the other side some of the names in the book will be changed to protect her and her family that she loves to infinity and beyond.

Our special angel-Felicia (we will call her) who reaches from the other side to touch the lives of all of God's children has asked with the guidance and help of God (Jesus), Mother Mary, Princess Diana and so many other beautiful angels has asked for a last wish to be planned and carried off with grace and love.

This project is for a learning center to be built. A learning center for children with learning disabilities of all types. Cerebral Palsy, ADD, ADHD, Bi-Polar, Mental illnesses of all types and severities.

Felicia wishes for a special earth angel to reap in the rewards of her own faith in Jesus Christ our Lord-God and Savior. A child who has faith and love within her own family. She is a special earth angel who will need on going care for her own special needs. She is a four year old girl named Ayla Faith. Ayla Faith has Cerebral Palsy and was born with a rare heart condition and also has had eye surgery all at a very young age. Ayla Faith will need special care for the long term and it will take much help to give her the teaching that she will need throughout her lifetime.

The need for special children from Maine and beyond is great. God himself has given His blessings for the learning center and has touched this project with love, hope and faith....

Ayla Faith's Learning Center is a wish come true for one special angel taken too early and the sales from this book will be 100% profit to the learning center. The dedication will be in memory of all missing and exploited children from Maine.

Felicia is a lost soul who wishes to connect with her family to help ease their pain. The learning center is her gift especially for her Mother. A woman who is missed dearly from the other side.

Love Letters in the sand-Ayla's Faith is communication between a special angel and two wonderfully God centered women. Co-founders of Lost Soul Spirit Connections. This book will help skeptics and even nay-sayers to help understand the love that mediums and light workers have in order to communicate with special angels from the other side.

Enjoy the love story as it unfolds and heed the great messages and the process of my learning who I am after many miracles among chaos in my own life. This is truly a gift straight from God and all of His angels that have worked miracles every day for generation after generation.

The pages that you are about to witness are a journey of pure love with Felicia communicating with Bella Louise (myself) and Cora Labelle. These are messages of love for this special angel's mother and family. A cry if you will for justice for circumstances beyond her control.

Believe it or leave it are words that I am given from the other side. Keep His faith and love this story for it is all He asks of us.....

Bella Louise Allen

Prologue

Just the beginning

October 29, 2015

> *Life seems to bring us what we need when we need it most.*
> *I have a wonderful story of love, faith and trust. It is not your normal*
> *Love story. The story I have to share with those who are willing to open*
> *Their hearts and minds is my journey finding God.*

Love Letter's in the Sand-Ayla's Faith is not just an extension of my heart to God's but an extension of a passion that goes deeper than anything I could ever imagine.

My second book in a series will show you how my journey with God and labeling with mental illness has not only affected me and my own family but the possibilities of how it has affected millions of families everywhere.

I suggest for more understanding on Love Letter's in the Sand- Ayla's Faith that readers check out my first book written "MIRACLES AMONG CHAOS". It will help shed a light for all to see in the book that I present to you here.

I hope to show how my journey with God and all of life's dramas and traumas can affect someone's state of mind as well as how an awakening can change your whole world.

Mental illness and dis-ease is over riding our country and even our world. I hope to shed a little light and understanding on the subject by walking you through the love letters that I have left in my own sands of time "LOVE LETTERS IN THE SAND".

Please enjoy my journey and remember we are all in this together to learn from one another and all of the tragedies and hidden miracles that

God sets before us. His plan is only to make us more loving and more compassionate human beings. May God's love and pure white light be with you each day and may you share your light with those who you meet.

Bella Louise Allen

Innocence Of The Child's Voice

Dedicated to "Sweet Pea"

Her words are barely audible at times
Sweet, wet, slowly they come
I struggle to hear her syllables afraid to let her know
"I'm sorry." "I couldn't understand."
The crooked grin that creeps across her lips and your heart seems
to burst with the love that such a small gesture makes.
I sweep the hair from her eyes so she can see the love that shines
from mine. This is the only gift you feel she will ever truly need.
As you snap that priceless photo in hopes of
freezing time right where it stands.
Her skin is as pure and white as the dove that Noah
sent to find the twig after the big flood.
Wondering what someday may come for her and for
you. It stops your heart just for one moment.
We must all have faith.
Faith that His love will shine bright enough for us all.
For what else in life is there, than that sweet sound.
The innocence of a child's voice.

AYLA FAITH
Meme loves you to infinity and beyond
November 14, 2015

Faith's Beginning

Hi, my name is Bella Louise Allen and I was wondering, have you ever had that nagging feeling to do or say something until you thought you would jump out of your own skin? Well, this is that moment for me. In my heart I have always known I was meant to write. It is something that I would put down for a while, yet I kept returning to it time and time again.

My life has not been an easy one, but the one thing that has kept me going is my unending love for the Lord. I am by no means a bible thumper. I am just your ordinary, run of the mill, American girl.

It is by life experiences and lessons learned that I keep turning back to God time and time again.

I was first introduced to the idea of God when I was three years old. I first attended our small town Baptist Church. It wasn't filled with spectacular stained glass windows or have a huge organ for filling the church with beautiful music. What it did have was good God fairing neighbors.

I remember the little white church with its steeple and big bell. This was one of my favorite parts about this little church. The bell would sound "Dong, dong, dong". All the children would come running into the church and look around for a familiar face to sit next to and listen to the Pastor as he gives God's message for the day.

I was the youngest of five. My brothers were Andy and Robert and my sisters were Eva and Amy. We attended Sunday service with our neighbors. Our parents were believers but not goers. Once we got to church we would split up and sit with our closest friends.

The day I fell in love with Jesus was the day I first saw him. It was truly love at first sight. His portrait was illuminated by a soft glowing light. There was a canvas painting overlooking the church. He seemed to be looking straight into the eyes of the whole congregation. It was as if no matter which seat you sat in his eyes were talking to only you.

My favorite memory of this church was the night we celebrated our dear Savior's birth. It was December 1970 and it was a cold stormy night. The snowflakes coming down I swear were white and pure as the wings of angels. I remember all the children and the excitement of getting ready to present our version of the Savior's blessed arrival. There were wooden hand carved barnyard animals. A donkey, a lamb and a cow. There was a small scale lean-to for the barn. The older children played the parts in the presentation as the three wise men. Mary and Joseph were played by my childhood friends. There was a beautiful baby doll with light brown hair and pink cheeks dressed in a long white gown with gold trim cuffs. Baby Jesus was lying in a cradle that the Pastor had provided for the Christmas plays for years.

I was so excited to be part of the choir. I learned quickly to appreciate the tinkling of the ivory keys. I may not have known all the words to "Away in a manger", but I would watch the other children and what I didn't know I would move my lips as if I did.

After our musical performance we all celebrated. There were lots of presents under the huge tree. We had strung popcorn and cranberries for the tree during Sunday school. We had our own personal Christmas ornaments made from the heart with Popsicle sticks, green and red yarn and we put our names proudly on our gift to baby Jesus on his birthday. The tree was adorned with various shapes and sizes of the hand cut snowflakes covered in silver and gold glitter to make the tree shine bright.

This is one of my finest memories of exploring my religious beliefs. At the tender age of three.

It was difficult to stay close to God, when the parents that you were born from, didn't practice their faith. Somewhere along their journey it got lost. Lost in the work, lost in the pressure of it being forced upon them as a child or just losing their faith in themselves.

If there is a will there is a way. I remember attending many other churches throughout the years. I attended the Pentecostal Church across from my grandmother's house. I loved that church, but not for the reason I should have at that age. It was all about receiving a gift. For every friend you brought to church you could pick a prize out of the treasure chest.

To look back on it I find that to be immoral. Although from the eyes of the Pastor he was trying his best to get the people to the church to hear God's word.

This was the church where I saw my first Baptism. I must say it was a little intimidating. To watch a grown man or woman stand in this big tub of water and get dunked under water. It scared me to death at that age. I now understand what was happening and it isn't such a horrifying thing as it was to me at the age of seven.

My next memory of attending church was when I joined my grandmother's church. The Catholic Church right next door to her house. The church itself wasn't bad but the service itself could be confusing if you didn't have a clue as to what you were doing. The sitting, standing, kneeling and singing was a constant work out when you attended Mass. I however kept finding myself coming back repeatedly from the time I was eleven to the present day.

In my late teens I even contemplated becoming a nun. I went to watch a young girl get sworn in. It was such a beautiful process. She seemed so peaceful with herself and the life she had chosen. That was something I had dreamed of for many years. I guess the very reason I sought out God and His light was so that I could have a great love and peace in my heart that I couldn't seem to find anywhere else.

As my life seemed to change from childhood to puberty and then to adulthood the one thing that never seemed to change was my search for peace. Peace and harmony in my life and a calm and strength within myself to go on through each day.

After surviving child abuse, mental, physical, emotional and sexual abuse I quickly got married and had children. I was doing what felt right to me at the time and yes everything we do is not without a purpose or a plan. I feel deep within my heart that all we live through and do is a lesson in God's plan for our growth. Whether that lesson is self-love, to help us teach our children better, to make us grow stronger in faith or to help lead us back to Him again. There has been a plan for us before time began.

My married life was not that easy. The older I got the harder my life seemed to get. It was like I was going backwards in the learning process. The man that I fell in love with was disconnecting himself from a woman he never really knew. I don't think I ever really knew myself at that point.

I was a stay at home mom for five years and I started to want more. What I wanted I wasn't sure of. I felt like I was going to crawl out of my skin if I didn't have somewhere to go. Somewhere to grow. I found some escape from motherhood and being a wife when I went back to school and started a part-time job. It seemed really great.

I thought I was tired as a stay at home mom. That was nothing compared to working part-time, going to school full time and then raising three children and a husband.

For many years I would wander aimlessly. I wandered from job to job and nothing seemed to be enough. I would spend money as fast as it would come in and that only put a bigger strain on my marriage.

I tried to "love" my children more than I was "loved". I was buying them everything I thought they needed or wanted. Little did I know I was only setting them up for disappointment in the early teens and young adulthood?

I started my own business with the intentions of getting out of debt and making a better life for all of us. I had no idea money couldn't buy the love of my children or my husband and it definitely couldn't buy our happiness.

I think back on the love that we did keep for one another through all the chaos that was present with the workaholic mother who was on the brink of a mental breakdown. The alcoholic father who was doing the best he could with what he had learned from his own journey as a child. My oldest child Mary Ann, I drew strength from. She was the rock that held me together. My oldest son Billy was a picture image of myself. I saw love and caring beam from his smile as he looked for acceptance from all. He was showing signs of something, I just couldn't put my finger on it for many years. Then my youngest son Corey was just trying to survive all the chaos he was born into. It was a really rough road for all of us.

When you bring two people together, marriage can be life altering once the marital union comes together and procreates. You may think you come from two different worlds, when in fact you have lived a life that mirrors one another.

There was rampant alcoholism on both sides. There was child abuse, numerous devastating deaths and the lack of faith all playing a role in how we made our choices based on learned behaviors. Those choices in turn impact the lives and choices that our children make. It all seems to be a vicious cycle. Like it or not it is what has been planned for each of us for a very long time.

It is up to us to learn from our lessons or to push them aside and keep on struggling against the wave of life's tide. Only we can change our lives. For the good or the bad. We have control of what we let happen and what we change.

Love Letters In The Sand

I feel your sweet breath
Pushing me, guiding me
I write letters in the sand

My heart swells to over flowing
Each day is like spring
I hear His wondrous song
I write letters in the sand

The sea gull soars high above
He soars the land for that which sustains
I write letters in the sand

Follow my words if you can
I will show you His love
I write letters in the sand

2.14.16
Bella Louise Allen

Moving Past the Pain

During my entire life there has been an inner struggle. No one knew it but me and God. It showed up in everything I did and with everyone I met. This struggle nearly took my sanity.

It is currently November 12, 2015 and I have never looked more forward to Christmas than I do this year. I have never been more at peace with myself and all that I am. My children are struggling that old struggle that we all call life. They are doing it to the best of their knowledge. I try to be there for them when I can. I hope that somehow I was able to teach them all that I could while they were in my care. The rest I have to leave up to God.

I used to be ashamed at the fact that I had three mental breakdowns. Those breakdowns were labeled as Bi-Polar II, Bi-Polar I, and Bi- Polar I with PTSD. I never really had an issue with going to the hospital for 9-14 day intervals. It was like a vacation for me. It was the only time that I actually got to rest and write and be me. I know that seems strange. I thought I feared it back in the day. I just feared all the obligations that I had. I was letting so many people down. Even in the darkest days of my life I was still worrying about everyone else.

While I was trying to figure out what was wrong with me during these breakdowns, my family was falling apart. I believe it was falling apart just as fast with me there as it was without me, so it didn't really seem to matter. The longer I spent in the hospital the more I saw that life could go on without me and I think that was my biggest fear.

I used to plan my funeral. Who would miss me and who might show up to my funeral. Who would cry or would just not really be affected at all. I know I had extreme depression. Who wouldn't with the workload I was putting on myself and trying to be super mom and super wife? The only question was when would it happen?

My first breakdown occurred in 2006. It hit me like a ton of bricks. I was diagnosed with Bi-Polar II. Looking back I only wish my children didn't have to experience it. Not having me around with my busy schedule was one thing but to be hospitalized for a mental illness was devastating, confusing and scary. There is such a stereotype with each label that is slapped on any one person with mental illness. It has become common place over the years to quickly judge the outside of each person's perceived symptoms.

If there is one thing I would like to change is how the medical field goes about putting the labels on so freely to all the young children and then the adults as well. I know it doesn't include every single case, but I believe it does include a great deal more than what the medical field believes.

I was hospitalized again in 2007. This time I was diagnosed with Bi-Polar I and my life had not changed one bit. I was on an antipsychotic medication and lithium. These two medications together with my depression and lack of understanding as to what had just happened was the most devastating thing to ever happen to me. I believe it was even worse than the child abuse that I had suffered. It had broken my spirit and my will to even want to get out of bed.

Things were a little different in 2014. I was divorced and trying to settle in to a new life. I had a near death experience a year and a half earlier and I yet again found myself searching for my reason for being on this great big blue planet. I had started to experience what I call an awareness. An awareness of everything around me. For the first time I was starting to appreciate the gifts that God had put before me.

In June of 2014 with my new found awareness I had experienced a vivid dream and shortly after that I was receiving "messages" if you will. Messages from songs on the radio, license plates, signs, the newspaper and even the television. I couldn't quite grasp what was going on. This would continue for about three weeks. One day when I went shopping I was hearing the first "voice" I had ever experienced.

"Erica." "Erica." While I was shopping it would get louder and louder as I got closer to the door it continued to get louder, "Erica". In amongst the hair standing on the back of my neck, unnerving, unforgettable, almost screaming throughout the store. I looked around to see if anyone else was hearing the same thing that I was experiencing. I also had an over sensitive hearing to the whole store. As I stood in the produce section the overwhelming noise of children talking seemed to fill the store. They, however never drowned out the sound of "Erica." "Erica."

In my fear and my inability to understand what was happening to me I admitted myself to the hospital. This was my first time I was actually aware of what was happening to me. I may not have understood what was happening, but I did realize I was however hearing "voices". Looking back on this, I wasn't actually hearing any one person's voice. It was just a knowing. A sense that I was awakened to things around me that I didn't understand and couldn't logically explain.

Since my three hospitalizations for mental illness, my near death experience after surgery, losing my father after a long illness and then witnessing the miraculous birth of my precious grandson it seems that my life had grown ten- fold and there had been an awakening that I still was not completely aware of.

As things seemed to change mentally and emotionally for me I started to know a sort of peace that I had never felt before. I was happy in my relationship. I was watching my children's lives form. It may not have always been the best of choices they were making but it was the choices that they were making that were helping them learn their own "life" lessons.

I was still struggling with my addiction to pushing myself to the limits. I still had one full time job as a caretaker for the mentally and physically challenged. I was still cleaning up other people's messes. By that I mean, I was still running a successful cleaning business. I was putting the finishing touches on my memoirs that had taken me over ten years to consciously try to write and to make sense of it all. With nothing but good intentions, I was trying my best to help all three of my children with any and all dramas or financial situations that would arise.

I was taxed to the limit. Mentally, physically and emotionally drained. I have no one to blame but myself. It is who I have been since birth. I am a healer, nurturer, and my needs have always come last. I wouldn't have it any other way. I have just felt unworthy of any self-love or nurturing for the things I needed. I don't feel it was truly anything anyone could fix or could have prevented. It is what God has mapped my life out to be.

In doing so I have learned all the lessons that I needed to prepare me for my next step on this great big spinning planet that we call Earth.

Learning To Fly

Dedicated to "My inner Child"

I see the wind floating, swirling all around me.
I turn right and then I turn left.
My head falls to my shoulder and an undeniable feeling overcomes me.

As I learn to let go, learning to fly.

My arms outstretch to touch the sky far above my head.
I turn faster, my feet barely keep the pace.
My eyes open for a moment to watch the world go by
Spinning, spinning, spinning.

As I learn to let go, learning to fly.

Overcome by the wind flowing through my long blonde hair.
There is a giggle that erupts from somewhere deep within.
My head swims and my eyes struggle to catch up.
Then the moment hits. A memory of the past overcomes me.

As I learn to let go, learning to fly.

I crash to the ground.
My breath is rapid and deep.
The plush green grass that sticks to my cheek brings me back.
I am back to the realities that I struggle with all my life.

As I learn to let go, learning to fly

11.25.15

Holding His Light

Time is precious and nothing teaches you that better than losing someone you love.

In my struggle to keep my sanity, my connection with my family and my numerous jobs I struggle with my faith with Jesus. My creator and Savior all in one. He first touched my life when I was three years old. I fell in love with His portrait on the wall. He brings me to my knees when I am only 9 years old with the death of my first love. A kind loving soul. He was sweet and pure of heart. Brian had a smile a mile wide. He was long and lanky and he had his signature Elvis hair do. Everyone knew I had this crush. I was teased horrifically but I didn't care.

The day God needed him most I found out what a cruel world we lived in. I didn't understand all that it would entail. To lose such a young man in such a tragic way.

A hunting accident in the fall of the year.

The snow was fresh on the ground and the air was crisp with a fog as each breath went in and out. The two teenage boys just barely 16 alone in the woods to find their kill.

The day had been long and the early afternoon darkness crept in. Rough housing and running and then "BANG". A shot rings through the air. A piercing sound that haunts my dreams still today.

Nothing could be done. It was already written. His fate had been sealed the day he was born.

This would be the first of so many tragedies in my life.

Seer ship is given to me. A word I find jumping from the pages of one of the many books that fall from the sky into my lap. I find it in the Bible.

A book I bought for .25. The woman who had it before me was Baptized in LE Mesa California August 16, 1953 Trinity Presbyterian Church by Rev. John R. minister. It is the most beautiful Bible I have seen. Its leather bound cover is cracked and worn. The ribbon is still intact and I use it as I am guided in my journey to find God's word daily. For inspiration in the morning and to help me understand my journey for that day. I hold my favorite prayers in wrinkled paper between the pages and precious photos of my loved ones. A true treasure for me straight from Heaven. Thank you Jesus.

Seer ship is given to Cora. My son's girlfriend. Another earth angel placed before me and my family. She has had her gifts of seer ship since the age of ten. A true blessing to her family. As our families merge and learn to love one another she and I join in our seer ship. October 2015, we form "Lost soul spirit connection".

We are given messages over much time. Messages that need to be part of this book. To show faith in Jesus. The messages are deep. We all are light workers. We are given puzzle pieces to put together for the big messages.

The messages we receive are gifts from God. Much pain has been given. The lessons are too deep. He is sorry for all the pain.

Cora and I are a work book in progress. We are his light workers for all to see.

I have been handed the word Pastoral Care. I see greatness and abundance in healing.

I see a documentary. I know how to manifest this and I see it go into the universe. A vivid blue illuminated dot. I am amazed. It will take patience and time and many light workers.

The message Casey is at bat. My neighbor. A young man in pain. It is his time to learn many lessons. He just lost his dad. A tragic loss and I know there will be healing when its time.

He is a mirror image of my youngest son Corey. I fear the same fate for him as I do my first love. I ask what can I do? Pray and give it up to God. It is in God's plan. He will have to learn his own lessons. Make his own choices and pick himself up by his boot straps.

How do I let go?

How do I sleep?

How do I, not do the work?

I was given a script straight from God. Date: 2.22.16. Rest often, every day. Rest every hour. Pray and let God handle it.

I have been given permission to write this book. He needs help. His children are suffering much pain and loss.

All I need is God and time. I will pay it forward to so many. I will pay it forward to those who accept my offer.

During meditation throughout the span of this lifetime. He comes to me in a white globe of beautiful LOVE. Yes, Jesus. Believe it or leave it.

He asks me "wake up" "open your eyes".

I say "I don't want to".

I open my eyes. I see better when they are closed. My third eye works better than my seeing eyes.

I see white light, blue dots, wings, animals, holograms, and coloring books for adults. (I want to take a picture-I can't) (I want to draw a picture-I can't).

He loves me as I love Him. He gives me my wings and they are gold.

I realize what I have received.

My heart hurts. It swells with pride. It is an awakening for the first time to all of His love.

His children. I have it when I hold my grandson. I have it when I connect eyes with my boyfriend. A love never ending.

After I wake from dreamtime I feel blessed. My head aches.

There is a band. An invisible band. I have felt this before. The doctors asked me in the hospital did I feel like I had a band or a ball cap on my head. I lie and say no out of fear.

I lied about hearing voices. I lied about hearing God. I lied about hearing His angels. Hearing His messages. Seeing His light and His signs.

I want them all know. That I do. I am His light worker. His See' er.

It doesn't matter if they believe. It only matters that I present it.

My book #2 LOVE LETTERS IN THE SAND-Ayla's Faith. A journey with Jesus. I walk and tell Him all of my fears, hopes and dreams.

It doesn't matter how many believe. What matters is that we do. The light workers. We will work daily to keep our own faith and to touch one life at a time. Open the door for those that need His love, light and His kisses from heaven.

Honoring His Name

I see many spectacular visions. I have extra-ordinary dreams. Astral plane dreams and vivid dreams. Why me, my unending LOVE for His presence in my life since the age of three.

I have seen Apollo.

I have seen Michael.

I have seen the head of Jesus several times.

I have seen the crown of thorns.

I have worn the crown of thorns.

I have had bloody matted hair.

He looks away. I am uncertain if it is in shame or sorrow!

I cry. I feel His pain. I have a new sense of the word empathy. I feel humbled. Loved and blessed.

He tries to convey I will be good. No matter what. My fear! I see myself collapse at his feet. I am Mary- Just WOW!

I sit and try to process this I hear and feel my heart beat throughout my entire body.

Am I for real? I have the crawlies on my left scalp. From the Left base of my skull to the front of my forehead. This is confirmation.

I am hungry. I will go feed my Brown Bear, my mountain lion. I have had a huge revelation in my dream state.

The brown bear has come to me many times in my lifetime. In my wake time and dreamtime state. I fear the bear. He means strength and power.

The mountain lion is knowledge and poise. He is fearless.

I hear "sit still and just BE". I know I must stop writing. I must stop working. I must stop carrying His load. I must just BE. I will try.

This is huge and I fear the mental institute that I stayed at three times in ten years.

It's o.k. I cry as I see myself, yet again. Walking around the long desolate halls in another fiery hell from today and tomorrow. A fog engulfs my entire world. This was not HIS plan.

This is not the first and I will not be the last. A misdiagnosed case and lost in the shuffle of the medicine world. Labeled because they didn't dig deep enough. Out of control and crashing into wall after wall because of a childhood out of control. No one is at fault. We are all at fault if someone doesn't step up to the plate. Our children are our future and they will not have one if something isn't done soon. I see it written and He is scared. A world ending much too soon. Will you see the end or will we pull together for His sake and that of our children?

I see pictures of pain pulled deep from the depths of hell on earth. Many lifetimes go across my movie screen. My third eye while I sleep. I see drugs, abuse, fighting, killing, scorned, battered and hanging from a cross. Women burnt at the stake and men swinging from a tree.

My pain runs deep my love runs deeper. I am so hungry. I deserve to eat. Yet I crave to do well. To prove my love for Him.

I saw a woman tonight in dreamtime. She was a client of mine from two years ago. She had a relapse with cancer. A blood kind. Her husband also had cancer. She is gone. I see her in her bandana. She is beautiful. She has a full face and she says please show them. Tell them to just LOVE.

I want my books to proceed charities. How much I am not sure. Diverse charities. There are so many. How do you choose? I choose personal loss first and then it can spread from there. His LOVE is great and so is mine. Just a penny jar in the scheme of things I know. I hear one at a time and it will make a difference.

Surrender Me

As I struggle to sleep and surrender me. He shows me animals. I believe it is for the Bangor Humane Society. A charity to honor our animal friends. One I feel a great connection with. They may seem to be insignificant but throughout my messages with a missing child case. A huge case from Maine. I receive the black lab puppies. They represent the many who helped rescue her soul. She calls them "her band of angels".

The messages in the bottle if you will, lead Courtney and I here today. At 4:47 in the a.m. I try to surrender me and yet I still push forward to give this sweet baby girl release from her own tears. She won't rest until MOMMIE rests.

She shows Cora on Halloween "her mother" Trisha, Felicia's mother. Trisha is in her bedroom watching TV. Halloween is a fun wondrous time for all children. A tradition that started with spooks and ghosts. Turned into fun for all the little ones. This little angel who was taken too soon shows Courtney, her mother. She wants her to know that she was with her on Halloween. Bringing her a sweet treat from the other side. Smile MOMMIE I will bring many gifts to all of the children because of your love and faith in me.

Going back and connecting me to the lost souls here on earth. My first stay at the mental hospital 2006.

I sit in a lunch room and I see through a fog and haze so thick enough God retches his insides up trying to heal Himself. They are lost and can't find their way home. A local hospital tries to help me surrender myself to the evil that I was raised in and the chaos that my life had festered into. Out of control and not knowing where to turn.

It is not any one's fault. It is just a lesson for all of us. A wake up call. Will you answer His message and help me surrender the children today.

They receive many false labels because we fail to look deep enough into all of the possibilities of our own failings. It is so hard to look in the mirror and see our weaknesses.

After many years of soul searching of my own I still come back to where I started ten years ago. Sitting in a chair and writing my thoughts, feelings and my greatest passion. My love for all human kind. Do I know how it will end, no? All I know is in surrendering me, I surrender to Him. A new awakening maybe. If just one person wakes from my books it is worth one minute lost on this sandy beach. Closed in by a glass shaped figure. The hour-glass. Time doesn't matter in the scheme of things. The only thing that matters is love. So I stand before Him now and surrender me.

"Little Miss Felicia", the missing child who comes to me and Cora for over seven months. You are worth it. Ayla Faith you are worth it. Stephen James Allen Tyler and my new grand baby, Deanne Allen, you are worth it. All of His children who have lost their way. You are worth it.

Surrender Me

I see through all of this fog
The lights come down like lightening
When it strikes will you stand tall
There are holes everywhere I look
Empty and deep they fall to the core of the earth
When will you surrender me

I climb, I dig to the light, and my fingers bleed
The soil is under my nails, I smell it and taste it
Dark and cold all alone I climb
This hole I have dug is endless
Just as I feel I am making ground
I wonder when you will surrender me

My hands slip from all of the tears
With the fear of it all I fall into the darkest abyss
I fall, fall, fall, deeper as I do pieces of my life
Flash before my eyes
My arms flailing, a scream so loud I can't hear it
Lost in the darkness, when will you surrender me?

The wind twirls me first left and then right
My head spins out of control my eyes struggle to keep up
The fall into this darkness grips my very core
I can't seem to find my way, when will you surrender me

As I descend to the bottom of this hole I feel His hand
He takes mine I hear him whisper "I am here"
My breath catches in my throat disbelief sets in
He says gently "I have always been by your side".
"Follow me and I will surrender you."

2.16.16
Bella Louise Allen

Kundalini and Me

5/24/16

I walk and I reflect in nature. The only place where I seem to connect with myself. I can shut it all out. The voices in my head shut down and I am…. I center and come back to earth.

Last night was a very emotional and spiritually awakening experience yet again. I struggle with writing all that happens. I cannot wrap my mind around this whole experience and fears surface again.

My story unfolds sometimes in fast forward. Sometimes in reverse. When I need a vacation I end up in the hospital. A forced shut-down of my nervous system. An over load and a breakdown. I thank Jesus, for staying with me this time. Finally aware. Aware of all that is Holy.

Praising Jesus…. Something that I never have done to this extent. I have loved Him. I have craved Him….. Peace in my heart and peace in my head.

Fearing ridicule and judgement I still open up. I was asked to "PROVE HIM"….. I stand up and I reach to the sky! Please Jesus, give me strength.

My best friend, my lover and I connect on a level unimaginable. As I struggle to close the "Veil" I see a white package wrapped in a huge glittery RED bow. It falls into a sea of red blood. I struggle to stay in the moment as Seth makes love to me. I cannot seem to keep the veil closed. Connecting on a level with God that I can't put into words.

This brings me back to my vision with Felicia. The first time I saw her in the blackness as Seth makes love to me. My glasses sit beside me on the night stand and I am blind to the darkness yet Felicia comes to me.

She just stands before me. In my mind-I think…..Oh, sweetie…..I know immediately why she has come. Felicia conveys to me that "Daddy laid with me".

I struggle to write this, but I am guided to reveal all. Prove ME….

How much do you love ME? I see Him and hear Him. He whispers many times in the past few months. 'HOW MUCH DO YOU LOVE ME"….

How do I deny Him after my vivid dream over 2 years ago? Jesus was calling me yet again to save those He has created. The reason for the season and the reason for taking the lives of the innocent.

A lesson in the blessing.

Will we ever learn? "Please" Jesus "Let them stop".

I stand before Him humble yet again…..I am but one woman in a world of despair and I expose myself as an imbalanced, labeled Bi-Polar, PTSD human. I cannot conceive this. How will they?

Slipping Through the Veil

I slip in and out of this thin line, the veil
I dance, I read, I sing to the heavens and then….
I ground…..

A beetle bug of shiny green lands on my chair…
Debbie, Roxie, and Taylor enter my mind.

Hale is with me…. So many angels from the other side. I bring
my concert "if you will" outside…. I sit and sing quietly.
It hits me as I refuel with Chia Tea and cheese. I am bringing my
concert to the waterfront. I dance quietly and sing. As I shape shift
on my deck-I am the eagle….I am given the name Blake.

I laugh and say…Really? Quickly I am given Prince.
Another sacrifice for the good of ALL MEN AND WOMEN…

Poof my mind is blown away!!! As I try to finally except this journey and
go through an emotional rollercoaster that I hold to myself out of fear!!
I have cut myself off from those that I fear will judge me and my
journey. I shut myself off from two beautiful souls. My sister Amy and
my friend and hopefully someday, new mother-in-law Laurie.

They both bring fear to the surface for me with another
hospitalization. I cannot let myself down!! I am….. Worth all of
this and by God I WILL not let Little Miss Felicia down. I will
not let my FEARS eat me to the point of breaking ever again!!!
So through the day and evening I try to rest when I can
and I rejuvenate my spirit, my body and my mind.
God is ever present now. The veil is lifted and I feel His presence along with
ALL of Felicia's Angels and my own angels. An amazing mind blowing
experience. I haven't shared these past few days with anyone. I need to trust
up and ask for Divine Intervention on a level that is beyond comprehension.
Thank you Jesus, thank you angels and thank you ALL that is Holy!!

Pure of Heart

Seth is…. My love, my life and my Light….. He is the beacon that brings me home and I am grateful.
Praise Jesus!!

Words that I have spoken to his mother. Laurie. Thank you for your sacrifices. Thank you for your gifts.

An amazing night of love and light. Thank you honey….

My dream time I see things…. My 3rd eye it is like a movie….. Slow it down, listen, feel it and then open your eyes. Thine eyes are open.

The rock of Gibraltar…. I saw it yesterday as I walked my path. The road that I gave up everything to love him. The road that leads me back to salvation……….

I close my eyes tight…. I try to stop my movie screen as he makes love to me…. The rock of Gibraltar…. He is Seth. I come home as I become one with him. I look up after I see the rocks… I try to figure this one out…. Pebbles, cannons and it hits me….Rocks.

Shortly after this vision I see His cross is being risen…Our sacrifice to the world. Exposing our love to all of His creation for the good of all man/woman/child… while he makes love to me like we have never laid together before.

He feels it and yet he struggles to look me in the eye….I ask him to please see me as I am….. He already did.

He loves me and I love him. We are a sacrificial lamb. One for the other. A Cinderella story for one another. My God I love this man more than life itself. I would give it all up for him all over again.

I write poems from the heart......
Deeper than dead.....
"How much do you love me...? "word" LOVE....

Just do it!!! Feel it with all of your heart. Breathe it in and just do it.

I wake up and I can't find my water. I have been searching for so long for His salvation.

He brings me another memory......... Oh, my Jesus!!

I am walking the desert.... 40 days and 40 nights... (The cartoon with Adam Sandler...I have been trying to place its title for the past two days).....
Finally I have walked across the burning sands of time. My poem that I wrote (? Time?????) Doesn't matter.
The Burning Sands.... My passion has come to light and I believe it? Do you???? It doesn't matter because Seth believes me and loves all of me.

The twin towers...... He is my twin flame. Brought to life by a passion of carrying the cross.
I put the cross down and I choose life.
I change my choices....
I choose life over death.....
I choose to LOVE HIM...
I choose to love me...
I choose to love Seth above all else on earth.......
My children have to come next and then my grand babies.......

The commandments to be brought back.
The songs will lift us up.
Glory will reign again.

PRAISE JESUS' NAME!!!

Passion of the Christ

Another emotional day and yet I am grateful and feel His love beyond comparison to any other.

I spent a little time with my grandson today.

What I suspected for a few days now is now confirmed. Praise Jesus' name!

Felicia I am so sorry this is taking so long. I hope I am doing the right thing and I hope for the children still here that your life can be for its intended purpose.

As I visit with my grandson I am guided by my band of angels and Felicia's angels. Just to watch and interact with Stephen- Meme's hero. A very special soul sent to teach all who have contact with him while he is here.

As he plays and interacts with me and my daughter I see his angels teaching him to be all that he can be.

Chelsey's grandmother comes to me. She is working with Chelsey to help get this HUGE message across. I know in my heart now there is no turning back. My fears are correct.

Stephen shows me what Felicia ate last for her "LAST SUPPER". She had spaghetti or spaghetti O's.

As we interact and all that is coming through is confirmed through my angels and the band of angels that works for Felicia.

Stephen shows his mother, father and I how his angels are working through him. He is intelligent beyond his years. He moves faster than he should and shows me what a true "MIRACLE IS".

Stephen confirms for me that I was wrong. Felicia was not poisoned by mouth.

Sweet Jesus', it was by injection. Just like she told Courtney. Oh, my God please have mercy on his soul…..

There is so much to this beautiful love story and I fear I won't be able to sustain the energy or passion like HE did.

I fear for my sanity to go flying out the door. I fear never to return to myself again. This is huge and I need help~!!!!!!!!!!!

I am shown by Sam, his manifestation that his mother is trying to convey. I don't explain anything I just take in the information and log it in my memory and my heart and my angels and God will help me to retrieve the information that is to be conveyed to be written. In the never ending LOVE story. The STORY OF MY LIFE!!! Not MY life….. But that of this world.

A story that is bigger than me and I ask the universe to send me the help, guidance and proper professionals to make this HUGE mistake right.

Miss diagnosis of mental illness, miss diagnosis of fear, miss diagnosis of hate, miss diagnosis of lust. The list is endless and if we don't figure this out together this will be the END!!!!!!!!!!!!!!!!!

Who am I

Who am I
I ask you again
Who am I

My soul bleeds every time I slip away
The price I agreed to pay
Each time I step into these shoes

Too big to listen to the me inside
I struggle on and on
I ask you again
Who am I

I choose your love this time
I will grow and I will learn
These ghosts they return time and time again
I walk my path the one that I agreed
I am only that, I am

Bella Louise Allen

Sacred Heart

It beats to a different drum can you hear it
This sacred heart of mine
I feel it under my feet as I stand in this golden field of wheat
This sacred heart of mine
The stream runs cool and clear run your fingers through its wet ebb and flow
There is a flame that sears to the core of it have you felt it
This sacred heart of mine
The thorns that pierce through its tender layers, taste the blood that drips from
its haunting memory
This sacred heart of mine
It belongs to you!
2.14.16
Bella Louise Allen
Happy Valentine's Day Jesus <3

Flesh

I AM FOUND FLESH DRIED AND WRINKLED
BLOOD STAINED HAIR MATTED TO MY FACE
YOUR EYES ARE CLOUDY AND I SEE INTO YOUR SOUL

THEY ARE JUST FLESH WOUNDS FOUND UPON THE SURFACE
MY BONES ARE BRITTLE BARELY ATTACHED AT THE SEAMS
SHE COMES TO ME TEARS STREAMING DOWN HER FACE
MEMORIES OF ME COME FLOODING IN

EYES NO LONGER CRYSTAL BLUE THEY ARE JUST EMPTY
SHELLS, SOCKETS WITH NO SOUL
MY PHYSICAL BEING LEFT THIS WORLD CRY NO MORE
I SACRIFICE MY LOVE FOR YOU
I WOULD DO IT ALL OVER AGAIN

THIS FLESH ONCE BURNED AND ACHED FOR YOUR TOUCH
AND YOUR LOVE
NOW IT IS GONE
DO NOT CRY DO NOT SHED ONE TEAR
FOR YOU WITH THE SOUL ON FIRE WOULD DO THE SAME
FOR ME!

As I watch Frozen the Disney movie the scene where Elsa is at the ball and is accused of being a sorcerer, witch or magician. I have a flash. A memory. A fear.

A past lifetime. I am Caroline. In my green velvet dress. It changes to purple. I am stirring the pot. A black cauldron with white fire. I am in the *mountains secluded. I die a young death. I feel I am being led by the left arm in this past life and others.*

I see myself. Burnt flesh. My eyes are empty sockets. I am laying down, dead. As if floating slightly off the surface of the earth. I see an abyss. I go from lifetime to lifetime as a witch, magician or sorcerer.

I then have automatic writing kick in and the poem FLESH erupts from my pen. I can't wait to put it to paper.

This is a pattern for my manic episodes with Bi-polar.......

I am not bi-polar....... I am experiencing memories from past lives........ What makes sense and what doesn't. I know in my heart it is true and real!!!!!! I am not crazy...........Thank you Jesus.

Waterfalls

The candle is bright flickering its golden hue
Silence is deafening and the dark is frightful
As I search for release. The water falls!

I hear your voice asking "why"?
I say "why not it's past due".
As I search for release. The water falls!

"Come to me". I hear within me
"Look into my eyes look deep".
"Do not fear me I forgive you".
As I search for release the water falls!

This mirrors image has grown old and weary
Is it too late, did I push too hard
Will I be able to save this child?
The girl who looks for release, release from the waterfalls!
2.14.16
Bella Louise Allen

Burning Sands

We are standing tall the two of us
Like the great eagle sitting high on his tree
His eyes pierce through us and he wonders why

We are greater than He. We are ignorant
We know not that what we do
Innocent until guilty

These walls come tumbling down
A towering inferno blazing for all to see
So many lost the grief reaches all shores and beyond

No mass of water can shelter this grief
No mountain can stop this pain
His heart sinks like the Titanic floating at the bottom of the ocean blue
An empty tomb with so many lost souls
They wander this world and beyond
Wondering when will the hate pain and fear stop

The great eagle looks down and a single tear falls
A memory of long ago comes
The burning sand from beneath his feet
The weight He carries is too much
Will you help carry the load?
Across this desert land

2.15.2016
Bella Louise Allen

Surrender Me

I see through all of this fog
The lights come down like lightening
When it strikes will you stand tall
There are holes everywhere I look
Empty and deep they fall to the core of the earth
When will you surrender me?

I climb I dig to the light my fingers bleed
The soil is under my nails I smell it and I taste it
Dark and cold all alone I climb
This hole I have dug is endless
Just as I feel I am making ground
I wonder when you will surrender me

My hands slip from all of the tears
With the fear of it all I fall into the darkest abyss
I fall fall fall deeper as I do pieces of my life
Flash before my eyes
My arms flailing a scream so loud I can't hear it
Lost in the darkness when will you surrender me

The wind twirls me first left and then right
My head spins out of control my eyes struggle to keep up
The fall into this darkness grips my very core
I can't seem to find my way when will you surrender me

As I descend to the bottom of this hole I feel His hand
He takes mine I hear him whisper "I am here"
My breath catches in my throat disbelief sets in
He says gently "I have always been by your side"
Follow me and I will surrender you".

2.16.2016
Bella Louise Allen

Losing His Spark

A tear falls down this solemn face
As I realize that I don't know all that I thought
This spark within me is as precious as gold
What ever would I do with myself losing His Spark?

This love I feel runs deeper than any canyon
Red as blood from the freshest of old wounds
As I try to embark on this wondrous journey
What ever would I do with myself losing His Spark?

I smell His sweet fragrance of violets and roses
A hint of the sweet masculine musk
My pulse quickens with just the thought
What ever would I do with myself losing His Spark?

I wait anxiously here in the dark
For my next thought
For this spark
What ever would I do with myself losing His Spark?

Anticipation of His love

I wait patiently in the darkest of night
I see the sparks I see His light
My skin tingles and my mouth is dry
In anticipation of His love

The candles are lite throwing there glow
There is a faint smell, a flower a rose
I see it in the dark waiting ready for bloom
My lips I lick in anticipation of His love

A Dream Come True

I wait anxiously trying to be patient
I have seen a vision a vision of pure love
It is bigger than me and bigger than you
My heart flips in my chest for the millionth time today
Do I dare "A DREAM COME TRUE?"

It comes to me again and again
I am taught Let that thing that you love dearest go
If it comes back to you it is yours
If not than it never was
Do I dare "A DREAM COME TRUE?"

It is like a tidal wave crashing to the blackest of rocks
The fear continues first high and then low
The jagged edges of those steep rocks cut my flesh
I bleed red warm almost a sweet taste in my mouth
Do I dare "A DREAM COME TRUE?"
He says "yes" it is time
A DREAM COME TRUE

Rising Out Of My Own Ashes

I am on my knees writing poetry
I am making plans for tomorrow
Not knowing how it will turn out
I am anticipating His love is great
I am seeing His love paid forward
I am healing so many lives
Young and old
Deserving and needed
I am grounded and good
I am ready for a new career
I have a career in the healing arts
A career in Seer ship
Thank you God
Thank you Mommy & Daddy
Thank you to my babies & grand babies
Thank you to my brothers & sisters
Thank you to all my friends & their loved ones
Thank you to all my ancestors from the past
My connections in the presence and my hope
My beacon for the future
Thank you Jesus
2.25.2016
Another visit from Little Miss Felicia. I love you sweetie. I have an early
Birthday Present for you and I hope mommie receives this message.
THUNDER ROLLS*-Felicia's Band of Angels*
I waken to another start as the thunder rolls
They are calling for help
Another one trying so desperately to waken the world

Bella Louise Allen

Can you hear it thunder rolls
The rain falls at a frightening speed
Wet and cold beaded on my window pane
They are crystals, Indigos and moon babies
The future
Our children
Can you hear them thunder rolls?
He has asked please
Hear the thunder roll
Mary is crying hear her weep
Feel her heart pounding deep within
Her hands shake and her body trembles
Can you hear them thunder rolls?
Dying faster from the inside out
It spreads like a plague
A curse from days gone by
Can you hear it the thunder rolls?
His eyes as deep brown as the earth's rich soil
They penetrate through mine
My own crystal child
My little miracle
I see him holding his ears
His steps are faster than they should
Way smarter than his years
I hear thunder
It's in his head
Help him to tame it
There is a fear in the night
Before it claims them all engulfing them like the fog
Dark in the night each one of us responsible for picking them up
Holding them tight
These special beings we call OUR children
He asks PLEASE hear the thunder roll
Bella Louise Allen
2.25.16

Copy written for LITTLE MISS FELICIA AND ALL OF HER BAND OF ANGELS…….Fly my little ones, fly!!!!
I FIGURE OUT OVER THE PAST EIGHT MONTHS THE BAND OF ANGELS SHE BRINGS WITH HER!
God
Jesus
Mary
(Higher powers that be)
I see Apollo in a dream/as I try to sleep
I dream of St. Bernadette
St. Michael
St. Raphael
St. Anthony
Hienriech Cornelius
Charles Fillmore

Earth my earth angels
And so many more taken too soon
Princess Diana
Whitney
Patrick
M. Jackson
Robin Williams
Kennedy brothers

I say thank you to all of my own personal angels
Powerful stuff!
Believe it or leave it!

Another sleepless night
I wake again at 2:15 a.m.
I am covered in sweat and my heart still won't stop pounding out of my chest
I tell her. "Felicia, I won't give up". "I will fight until the end". You're a baby girl as stubborn as they come. You make me smile and my heart warms me through.
My own babies keep me going. Keep me fighting for you.

Bella Louise Allen

Mary Ann, Billy, Corey.
Stephen
Ayla Faith
And my new baby girl!

On May 5ᵗʰ 2016
I send Mommie one more message!
Straight from you!
Hear her! Another sleepless night!!!!

November 14, 2015

Sgt. in Arms,

I hope you have had a chance to take in all the information that I have given you. Since our meeting additional communication has transpired and I wanted to let you be aware.

I have little control of when it comes, I just know I have to pass it on. I hope that you take in consideration my suggestion for learning or understanding how psychic or mediumship works. That is the only thing that will help you and your team.

I still have a barn that is being shown to me. It is still active. There are corn fields and posted signs. The barn is the starting point. A point of reference to finding her.

There is new information. I smell diesel fuel and see logging trucks. There is a four-wheeler with a cooler. I can't see it, but I feel she is in the cooler.

There is a logging road. I believe it is active. I see tires lots of tires. I see a gate or rope with markers on it. There are acres and acres of trees. Some are fallen some are standing. There is a big bank or a pit of some sort. I see trash scattered.

I still see a trail that splits. I believe this to be the road that she is down. I see a split and then it turns back. There is some kind of water. It doesn't appear to be a lot. It is like a small stream, brook or mud hole.

She is in a hole. Not very big. I see leaves and downed trees. I also see a medium to large size rock, not on top of but close to her. I hear fast traffic in the distance and slower traffic closer to where she is.

I believe this is all the information she has for me. Only time will tell, like I said earlier I have no control of what comes in only of what I have to pass on. I hope this is helpful and if you have any questions you have my contact information.

Thank you
Bella Louise Allen

Mt. Hope Cemetery

November 2015

It was only a few weeks that had passed that Little Miss Felicia had first connected with Courtney and me at our first case in Brownville.

I travel from home to my two jobs. I work as a direct support worker full-time and I run a successful part-time cleaning company. I have taken care of and cleaned up after people all of my life. A job which I wouldn't go back and change for all of the world. I am a caregiver and I love every bit of the choices that I have made over the years.

If I had not chosen to be the caregiver that I have become what would I have done?

At one point in my life I wanted to become a nun. I wanted the peace love and serenity that such a life style would have given me. That is just a part of why I feel I have been led to this point in my life.

My childhood traumas. My adulthood dramas. My near death experience and my pure love of God has brought me right where I belong. Standing again in front of Him with my arms outstretched and aching for His acceptance and grace.

I ask Him for forgiveness again and again. Yet, I know He already has forgiven me.

As Felicia tries to convey her needs and wishes she connects with me at Lost Soul Spirit Connections first case. She gives to me the name "SCOOBY DOO CREW". It was raining and dark and we were trying to help a woman who had suffered much tragedy in her own life.

In my travels to and from work I had passed Mt. Hope cemetery several times. I felt a draw, a pull, a desire to stop and visit the cemetery for some reason. Back in early November of 2015 as I was driving to my job. My sister

Eva calls and asks who is this little girl? Eva is at work and Felicia has come to her.

I asked Eva to describe her to me. She is small around the age of 4 and she has blonde wispy hair. I know right away it is Felicia.

In a split second it hits me. The cemetery and Felicia. I ask Eva to ask her if she will come with me. To the cemetery. Eva says Felicia stutters. She is excited and she jumps up and down and then Felicia is gone in a flash.

I have been listening to Paul Cardell's c.d. Miracles since the night of Lost Souls Spirit Connections first case. A beautiful song called "Voices" plays and as it does I feel Felicia enter the car. I get chills up and down my body from head to toe three times. A feeling I have never experienced in my life. I smile.

I smile and say "Hello, Felicia". My heart is pounding out of my chest and I know it is a feeling that she and I share in that moment. I feel her excited energy.

I feel she knows what I am about to do. I don't even think I knew what was about to happen.

I talk with her and as we enter the cemetery from the back entrance I look around and see the monument for the veterans and all the flags. This cemetery is one of the most beautiful cemeteries I have ever been to. We drive around and I talk to Felicia about the beautiful cemetery and I ask her if this is where she would like to stay until Mommy can find her body. I don't hear it or see it. I just know it is right. We wouldn't be together going to the cemetery if it wasn't what she wanted.

I parked the car out by the front entrance and we walked around the pond. I have a bag with things for this occasion. I had no idea why I picked these things up and didn't know why I was carrying them in my car until I got out of my car.

As Felicia and I walk around the pond there were lily pads in the pond and a few frogs. I am amazed because lily pads are something that she has shown me in the first few days of our communications.

I walk around slow and take in the lay out of the grounds. I ask Felicia where she would like to be put to rest. She takes me up past some of the fenced in headstones and we start to climb to the top of Mt. Hope Cemetery. I laugh because I knew where she was going and why.

Felicia wanted to be as close to heaven as she could be. I don't blame her. It was beautiful. I see red berries and white birch trees and tall trees and small trees and a huge bank. There are so many beautiful headstones. Really old headstones. I read through the names and dates and am amazed at how young some of the children where when they died. Nothing has seemed to change. It happened back then just as it does today. It doesn't make it any easier to know this. It just is what it is. Life.

As Felicia and I come to the middle section at the top of Mt. Hope Cemetery I feel the need to stop. I ask her is this it? It is. I turn to the left and there is a family plot. A huge stone is in the center. The name Learned is on the stone of this family plot.

There are three small markers. I feel these to represent Felicia, Mommy and Daddy.

I had in my car my homemade drum and my incense and a small ceramic figurine of Mary and baby Jesus. I had picked up some fake pinecones and red berries. I place the pinecones and berries into the ground and I place 1 incense by each marker.

I light the incense and I start to beat my drum. I ask for God's assistance with helping Little Miss Felicia to ascend to be by Jesus' side in Heaven.

I chant and I pray and I pick a verse from my special Bible and I kneel and pray. I pray for Felicia. I pray for Mommy and Daddy. Forgiveness is needed for all to be together again one day.

As I get up from my knees I find a pure white feather under my left knee. My job is done….She is with Jesus…. Believe it or leave it.

Felicia- October 30, 2015

As I was on my way to work I turned out of my driveway and a huge rainbow greets me. I smile and my heart catches in my chest. I say "good morning Courtney". I listen to my "Miracles" cd. I struggle to find the song I feel would make a great introduction to LOST SOULS SPIRIT CONNECTION- the documentary of our journey with lost souls searching for peace. The song is "Hearts are turning towards God". A beautiful song and the point of our whole mission is within the words. The instrumentals are eerie yet seem to touch the soul of the people searching for peace within themselves. The peace you can never find without His light shining in your heart.

As I reach downtown Bangor, Maine the sirens start. My ears are on alert and my heart fears for who may be in trouble. I see up the hill on Main St., police cars, an ambulance and a firetruck. I pull to the side of the road to let another ambulance pass. A wave of heat passes through my body and I let it go. I look for a place to park and there is one close to my job this morning.

As I get out of my car and unload, my interest is peaked with the accident just half a block up the hill. I stay focused on my job. It's none of my business. I worked on an ambulance for two years and they have it covered.

As I lug my cleaning supplies to the building, I see a gentleman in his mid-fifties. I see concern on his face, empathy for what may be taking place. As he talks to a gentleman that reminds me of Santa Claus he tells him, the car just flipped in the air. I hope everyone is o.k.

I struggle not to go to the scene of the accident. I stay the course with my job at hand. I go in to clean and I bring my stuff in through the door and I notice on the ground the leaves off the tree on the sidewalk have fallen everywhere. They almost look identical to lily pads. I am surrounded by lily pads. I however find one tiny lily pad (represents Felicia)

Felicia shows me over and over again today, Santa Claus…. She wants someone to find her before Christmas.

Cora had mentioned that Felicia told her about lily pads. Where ever she was there was water and lily pads. Hmmm???

I go to clean my stairwell and I vacuum a flight of stairs and I then find this twine. The same kind I have found before. To me it means there is an attachment of some kind to something.

I also found two rubber bands. One is a complete circle, the other is broken.

I feel Felicia is with me today. She is guiding me with many of the things I see. She has peaked my interest with what might be true of her disappearance.

While cleaning I see a map on the wall that I never noticed before. This is what stands out to me. The number 3. Propeller. (I question, anchor or weight). I keep getting drain or sewer.

When I go down stairs to vacuum I see 2 cigarette butts on the floor. ? Two people... or he was a smoker.

I come out and load my truck and I find shards of glass on the ground. My mind goes directly to drinking. Alcohol. —info. Found out after----(I think this is the accident up the hill.) (The windshield was completely broken out of the van).

Curiosity finally killed the cat. It finally got me. I have a pull, something or someone says go. Go to the accident. Ask the police officer about Felicia's case see what he knows. How can I get Courtney's information to them?

I meet the officer. I ask him about Felicia's case and he shares with me he doesn't know a lot about her case but he believes it is now a cold case. I said I think your right. I ask who I could get in touch with about her case and sharing Cora's spirit visit from Felicia. He said to call the local police department and they should be able to hook us up with the right people. The officer has Amber eyes. I ask is your name Kevin, he says no. I am Keith. I joke with him and tell him I don't have the abilities that Courtney does and we both laugh. He seemed like he believed me and was taking me serious. Thank you Jesus.

I feel relief after talking to Keith. As I leave a gentleman looking concerned was still watching them clean up the scene. I stop to talk to him for a second and as I turn around I notice the van has a completely broken out windshield. (It also has)- 492 Amy -license plate. Courtney said Felicia showed her

I -92 a double highway. Cora believes Felicia is buried in New Hampshire and Felicia helped her draw a map of where she is located. There is water and lily pads.

I tried to connect more deeply with Felicia today at my housekeeping job. When I asked her about things the only physical thing I got was a sharp pain in my right front forehead. I had gotten this earlier that morning.

Cora said Felicia showed her she was hit in the head several times and she was wrapped in plastic. I got from the map she was wrapped in a shower curtain.

Pray to Michael-
The man of 10,000 sound effects
Police Academy
Skunk-learning healthy boundaries… + more
Win----Slow????

I have found two tiny gray bird feathers with pure white in the center. One at the first job site and then another at the second job site. (? White center a kiss from heaven from Felicia- the outer edge is her family-gray/crying/sad/ broken hearted).

I stopped by my friend Missy's work place. Her husband is a Police officer. Her brother is the on the force as well. If anyone can get the information where it needs to go I believe she can. She and Carl both are aware of spirit and how some of this stuff can work. God, please help us to put Felicia's family at peace by helping the authorities find her body and a killer. Mother Mary help all those involved to bring peace to the family and friends and all the people who have cried out for your love and white light with her return. May this help just one person see the light that you shine so they may have peace within their hearts. Amen.

Cora connects with Felicia, missing for far too long.

Cora sends me a texts as she receives her message from Felicia.
Gouldsboro- a path that splits in and becomes 1.
She's with Jesus

Trees, water, and big trees.
She's scared when she takes me there, I'm very cold.

Blows to the head. She is wrapped in plastic.

I'm freezing, like I'm in ice. It's a river.
There is a big bank.

She's right next to the water. She shows me lily pads.

People have been so close but so far at the same time.

The number 96.
It's a west East sign
She is past where the trail splits then turns back into one and to the left,
by the river.

I drew it Ma.
She showed me what a map looked like and I just drew it.

I keep seeing a double lane like a highway. I asked her to show me what
the road looks like. But it's a highway surrounded by trees. (The undeveloped
east/west highway).
She's not in Maine Mom. She's in New Hampshire. I get it. Where she
is looks like here, but she's not here people have been so close but so far away.
She is definitely in New Hampshire.
The numbers are wrong and there is no town with that name, but I'll
get it.
Believe it or not you've heard of the east/west highway. They've been
fighting to build that. It connects Maine with New Hampshire and New York.
Well, that's the name of the interstate 92.

Some things matter…. Some things don't…. You tell me…..
You are going to need lots of dogs. Felicia says Black Labs. She showed me
black labs all day yesterday.
Felicia's birthday she shows me. I saw this on a calendar yesterday while
she was with me. She showed me signs.
The license plate on the van that got in the accident. It was the Maine
agriculture plate. Small child and an adult walking hand in hand away. They
are blackened out. (I believe this is Felicia walking away to the darkness with
her killer). She knew her killer!!

License # 492 (Felicia's birth day/month and I-92 East West Highway)

Windshield blown out… Her case is finally blown wide open. They can see where she is.

I look for information on the East/West Highway. Felicia tells Cora it is the first one.

3 possible routes considered undeterred by the FHWA's denial….
Felicia says its number one…
Southern Route- 452.8 miles from the area of Albany, New York to Calais, Maine.

This corridor would have required 181.2 miles of new construction and 225.4 miles of upgrading existing facilities. Approx. 462.2 miles would have utilized already existing Interstate highways I-393 in New Hampshire, and I-95 and I-295 in Maine. The route, which is estimated to cost $782 million by the time it was completed in 1979 would have gone through Bennington and Battleboro Vermont, Keene, Concord and Rochester, New Hampshire and Sanford, Portland, Bath, Ellsworth and Calais Maine.

October 31, 2015
Cora talks with Felicia again today and sends me her messages through text…
I can see what her mother is doing. Right now Felicia is with her.
This man stopped to get gas. He was wearing a tan jacket. Like a carhartt. When he got gas the letter S and he bought a candy bar.
It's a mobile.
She knows him.
Her mom knows who.

October 31, 2015- Bella Louise-me- I have a visit from Felicia.
I have a pain in my stomach that goes from my stomach to my heart. It lasts for several minutes. My intuition tells me, her mother knows Felicia's father killed her. Her mother feels responsible for her death. ? Was there a dispute between mother and father over Felicia? Was Felicia's father obsessed or pissed at her mother and preferred to hurt mom over his love for his own child???????
Her mom knows who did it.

Her dad knows too.

It was too hard, she said they hired someone.

The girlfriend knows. And no she is scared they are going to do it again she's crying.

(My question is, who is scared? The girlfriend?? Or is Felicia scared? Why would she be scared if she is already with Jesus?? Is she scared for herself, her mother, the girlfriend, or the brother???

It's a jeep.

Tan or white older Jeep like 90's.

9386

9386uv

He is going to believe me she just told me that he has been going nuts

I need to find out where the East West corridor is supposed to go that's where she is.

I said Maine, New Hampshire, Vermont, and New York. She is in New Hampshire.

It's a river not an ocean.

We need a lot more than black lab dogs Ma, lol but yes. We do. She is showing me a black lab puppy.

I'm seeing writing and tabs open. Like multiple things at once I see a map of water. (Felicia knows I am writing her case in my computer. She sees I have the East/West Highway information open. She is showing us the first option for the Highway).

Cora says-my ear feels full.

She said open your first... What's your first? (My first E/W highway option).

East/West Highway I-92- first choice out of three. Felicia says the Southern Route.

November 1, 2015

I'm at work and Felicia was with me in my dreams. I however can't remember what any of it was. I didn't feel bad or sad. I knew when it was time she would show me what she wanted me to know.

Shortly after dressing and getting my work underway. Pop…. I get a picture of how to get Felicia's killer, to get justice for her murder and disappearance.

She brings to me the girlfriend. No one was hired. Felicia's father is threatening her. Possibly with harm to her or her own children. That is why Felicia is scared. She fears if the girlfriend steps forward that someone else will be hurt or killed.

She shows me like an interrogation. I see pictures of my own children, pictures of Cora's daughter-Ayla. I see the table plastered with our little angel Ayla.

How can a mother keep this horrible information from another mother? Put her in Felicia's mother's shoes. Make her feel her pain. Let her look into the eyes of Little Felicia and still lie!

Felicia shows me Cora connecting with her in front of the girlfriend and her finally breaking. Giving up all the information she knows.

I feel, but don't know. If we can't find her, we can get justice for Felicia.

Bring peace to her mother and grandfather and family and town and police officers and the world.

She is with God and is at peace. She just wants mommie to be happy. She wants mommie to be able to see her little face again, smiling. Stop the pictures of the unknown. Trust in God's plan and I will see you again.

"Share this song with mommy and the world".

"Hearts are turning towards God"
A Journey of hope and healing
www.paulcardell.com 2007

Trying to piece it all together…. Box it up… step away….let it go.
I'm sorry sweetie. It's getting really hard.
No one wants to listen.

I won't give up on the center. Cora and I have started work on it today. We bought blue tickets for you and a Mr. Potato head. I got information for Wal-Mart. We can put a flyer in the break room but no donations anymore! We will figure it out. One step at a time. One day at a time.

I bought my sisters oil painting. I just had to have it. A photo of tranquility for you honey. I look at that and see you somewhere in the tall grass and your sitting. You close your eyes and squeeze them really tight. You make a wish. You have a beetle that has landed on you tiny little finger. You wish only for peace and love. Mommie is so sad and you watch her every day.

The sun beats down on your light blonde hair and its wisps fly in the air as you say it "I love you mommie" and you blow out your candles. A wish made without a cake.

As the day goes by I keep hearing and seeing- The lady in red- Julia Roberts- Cora asks you what does this mean….She says that was her favorite actress… Felicia keeps saying "FINE".… This is related to the movie Erin Brockovich … her son is mad because of the lack of attention and his mother is working too much. So, I think that mystery is solved!!!

Felicia keeps showing my TAYLOR----- She loves Taylor Swift… Say you will remember me!! Her favorite song.…

She shares with me though she wants to hear Adele's song "HELLO" often.

Felicia keeps showing my sign language. I'm not sure. I think this is a way for us to communicate with her from here. She may also may be conveying the curriculum at the center.

She shows me how to sign----communication in. communication out. Three middle fingers in. Kind of like bunny ears with the pinky finger and index finger. Pump your chest 2x and up to heaven… Then wiggle it. Yellow for the wiggle?

Brush the cheek with the thumb?

Finger tips to the chin and then out to the other hand? Thank you?

Felicia shows me a couple others. My sign language is not good at all.

2/26/16

Felicia takes me there

There is a cedar tree to the right of this tree is a small pond of water… not big

How deep???

She is here dig but not too deep

Thank you honey

She keeps showing me the Shaw House

Sarah's house

The house that jack built
Ayla's faith???
There were Cardinals 3x this week
Bam- I brush my teeth and I have Princess Diana come to my third eye.
I see her!
I am floored at her appearance. Again an angel with golden wings
A woman taken
A woman of pure love- on both sides
I instantly know…..
Princess Diana is helping with the messages for the dance and fund raising
for her center. The dances. The fun. The family. The love…. The faith…
Change!!!

She shows me books from heaven
Falling for the children
Falling for the teachers
She shows me a documentary
She shows me a movie
Nothing benefits one person
Every one gains wholly
Effort must be had in order to achieve HIS plan
Save HIS children
Start there
Start in Maine
Have Faith, work hard
Her love will spread like a wildfire
"If you build it they will come"
Schools, classrooms, values, love
A center- in her memory and the memory of all of Maines missing and
exploited children
Ayla Faith's Learning Center
A gift for all who need it.
She knows. Let her lead the pack.
A mother- bear-brown! Me (Bella)
She can make it happen. I know.
That's why you hear me whisper

"FROM THE OTHER SIDE"
Little Miss Felicia
Broken hearted
Mend it with love!

I wake @ 3:33
2/27/16
A message….
A new center to pay it forward you are given a gift today. See it no other way.
I see a sunflower- Many sunflowers.
Today will bring forth many miracles embrace them and trust Him.
For now is the hour to shine bright and show the world his gifts
The light workers
His little light
Please let it shine

Waking again after only a 40 minute sleep. Shaking and heart pounding out of my chest.
I try to write and I start to cough. I write…
Sunflower.
Mosquito
My Dad guided me to a gift the other day. For me I thought. It is for the center
A gift in HIS name
Because of all of my love
HE IS RISEN
Books many
For the children

The time is 5:59 On 2.27.16
I write:
He -1ˢᵗ
Me-
You

This equals change. (Period) Importance
Change- 5
Now for all the children around the world- (draw a globe of the world)
The 1ˢᵗ on the map is Maine

She keeps showing me #9=? To believe
FAITH/AYLA

Unimaginable

2:22 a.m.

I struggle in writing this… It was not a dream it was a nightmare. It was her nightmare. Did it happen more than once? I think once was once too many.

The bile rises into my throat and I can't stop the tears from rolling down my face.

Felicia shows me a horrific sight. She shows me the couch downstairs in the basement. It is covered in blood. Her blood. Even now she tries to tell me he didn't know what he was doing. I try to wrap my brain around it. How a man or anyone can hurt someone that they gave life to in such a horrific manner.

I keep seeing a screwdriver. I sense sexual abuse. I see her struggle but she was too little. She couldn't fight him off.

There are so many children that experience similar stuff as this. How do I let this go and still sleep? I am so tired and yet I still have this drive to get this message of eerie proportions to those who can help bring justice for Felicia.

If someone would just believe. Believe in her and believe in Jesus.

Situations such as this test our faith daily. There comes a time when we must take responsibility for our own actions. We are given a conscience to help keep us walking in His light. Some people use it as an excuse to do evil. This is one of those cases. To do such evil to an innocent child and then cover his tracks so meticulously. That my friend is premediated murder. Murder of an innocent child.

I may only be a woman with a heart filled with love for Jesus and all the gifts that have been given to me, but how do I sleep knowing the truth of this child's end of life?

Felicia shows me two trucks meeting. They park…. There are two men. One has a box on the back of his truck. She shows me snow and a trail. It crosses over a dirt/logging road. She shows me that it goes out past the store.

How far I am not sure. I feel it is on the right side. I see cornfields and a farm. This is just a starting point.

She has shown Cora and I railroad tracks and Bacon St. It is another starting point. There are old R.R. Track's that come to new tracks. She says-"so close yet so far". (TRACKS)?? She emphasizes tracks!!! She is close to the river bank. There is a cedar tree---cedar camp—cedar road….. There is a small hole, drain. The tree is the key… At the stump/hole? Is there a hunting camp on this property?

Things happened so fast. There was a lot of hatred and out of control behaviors.

Wow is all I can say. Is this a gift or a curse? It truly makes me wonder. I don't feel I give myself enough credit for all that she has shared with me over the past seven months. I couldn't make this up if I wanted to.

I have always hated horror movies and now I live in it almost daily. I feel blessed that Jesus keeps me strong and grounded this time. For how could I go to sleep each night knowing I will relive another horrific night of her torture? How could I wake up and still be forced to see the signs daily of her showing me. "Please help me".

She has asked me if she could call me… Meme. I fight back the tears and smile with pride and say "YES". She loves it. She twirls and giggles and my heart swells with pride. I never even met her and she fills my heart with love. Amazing! Believe it or leave it!!!!

Felicia's Faith

2/29/16

Felicia says good morning. Thank you to me again for all of my hard work. She is getting excited because she knows it will only be a matter of time before someone gets a hold of me to see the room. Her room full of treasures for her mother.

A letter to address it all. I ask her to come forward in my automatic writing. A form of healing and a form of love for those who will read this book. Felicia asks me to write her story. FROM THE OTHER SIDE. She asks to tell everyone to help them understand the love and faith it will take to heal from her tragedy. The loss has been one of great magnitude and God knows.

What does He know? He knows that something must be done soon and it must involve a great deal of His people.

Seven months ago after a case was solved with the LOST SOUL SPIRIT CONNECTION Felicia is brought forward by Cora LaBelle. A very gifted young woman. Cora did this after a test of our own faith.

Bella asked Cora to bring forward a gentlemen. She asked Cora through telepathy. A form of reading someone's mind. She was nervous but brought through within seconds who it was.

The man who Bella thought was an earth angel from the moment she met him. Her best friend's husband. (Charles) A man who appeared to her in a near death experience. (Read about this in her book-MIRACLES AMONG CHAOS) A book with connections to this book.

Cora brings him forward and starts to describe him. She starts out by describing him in ways that I would recognize him. She said she felt he was very handsome. Like my youngest boy. A chick magnet. She said Charles had beautiful eyes like my oldest boy, he was a lady's man. A kind soul that had come a long way in life from not believing to believing with all of his heart. A man wonderful with children and a loving husband and father.

Bella immediately knew Cora had a gift and it should be shared with the world. This would not be revealed for months later when Little Miss Felicia-me. I wouldn't stop invading the lives of these two women.

In my writing it gets difficult to know which angel helper comes forward for Felicia. She has a band of angels that are helping her. She is a very excitable angel and she is hard to pin down to get some details from.

In the evidential room- if you will -is a story to unfold. Seeing is believing and it must be done almost one piece at a time. It must be done with grace and love. Kindness and compassion and above all you must keep the Faith. Felicia's Faith!

Why Cora and Bella? Cora has a connection with Felicia through her own daughter. Cora knows this story but I will only show you a glimpse of it. Cora's daughter's name is AYLA FAITH! A name switched about a month before she was born. Ashely had it all set for Aubrey (I believe). Cora has started her own book. A healing too many years in the making. One of strict upbringing and a test of her own FAITH for all of these years.

No support from her own family. This story will be another book. Cora's story which will touch the lives of many later.

Everyone and everything is connected. Everything means something. Somethings mean nothing. Pay attention some of these things only mean I love you from the other side. How much faith do you have in Jesus? How much do you love me? She wants only healing from this tragedy. Don't make this about hate of any kind. Don't judge it believe it. Believe in me and especially believe in Him. For without Him we would not exist.

In the room is a box. A couple of boxes. A few bags. Stuff is displayed. Like a museum of the messages received to help those who have such a hard time to understand the worlds that really do exist beyond this big blue planet.

There is a story board. A vision board if you will. A vision that Felicia tries to give to her mother and family and then to the world.

She wants her life celebrated. Not lived in pain and agony. She wants a birthday party. She wants a ticket tape parade. She wants a masquerade ball. She wants a learning center in honor of her memory. Not her death. She wants it to be named after AYLA FAITH. She wants it to include old fashioned values. She wants it too represent love and laughter. She even wants God to be brought back to life for the children's sake.

She knows this world has come to a turning point where there is no faith left. He has a plan for all of us.

Hard as it seems it was.

In trying to get to this point with Felicia's story and trying to bring justice to her case. She and her BAND OF ANGELS- which is huge- have built a case for the public to decide if this is real or not. Help the LOST SOUL SPIRIT CONNECTION- THE SCOOBY DOO CREW. If you will. That is what she calls us. Bring her case to light and bring her home.

There is information within the pages of many sleepless nights for both Cora and Bella. A case built up because no one has believed enough in the evidence brought forward until now. The police where given documented messages from Felicia over the course of eleven days.

She now has given them more than seven months' worth of evidence. Who will be the one to step forward and listen and hear them out? Who will make my last wish come true?

Felicia wants to take a ride with Cora and Bella to the spot where she is buried. It is close to her home. Only time will tell and only Felicia's Faith will prevail if someone will hear her voice. From the other side!!!!!

Felicia Returns full force

2:02 a.m.

I had one night off and I hope that is not all she is going to give me. She knows I am going to see Katie tomorrow. My "teacher". I will ask questions only for guidance. I will still listen to my inner self and make the best judgement that I can.

In my dreamtime state I see it all over and over and over. I know what I should do with it but I fear that he will move her body. I get confirmation of this…. Shit….

Wow… I still ask was she shot…. I rustle with this one. Is it my own stuff coming through or did they really do it. I think it would be better than what I see in my third eye. Buried alive. Scratching to get out of that cooler.

I want to handle this with grace and love and dignity. I want Felicia's mom to step forward to help me with this and give the princess' and fairies a birthday party to remember. How do I go?

(WIN-SLOW) IF that even means to win slow. I remember her showing me win-----slow that day back in Bangor when I was headed for work. I wish she was older so I could just sit her down and say o.k. where to hell are you????

I wish Dad had a flipping conscience or the best bud did. Why the hell doesn't someone step forward…..

Dad needs help for God sake….. Confirmation of WHYYYYYYY? I can't give this up.

I still see "ask Joannie" for my colors……Does this mean ask the experts on whether they can pull her through or whether I need help to get better detail. How many people do I get to help me bring this child home……?

Source tells me to PROOF Him…. He tells me she IS in her hometown and I am the only confirmation I need. He tells me to go there and PROOF Him.

Felicia's Christmas List
Love above all else
Keep the Faith
Forgive all for they know not what they do

Keep her memory pure and full of love. Share the story of love, faith and forgiveness. Help those children who need it the most.
A list of her wishes. Believe it or not!
A ball for all the little princess'
Fill the room with fairies and princess'
Make them feel beautiful and loved
Make it a time for all mommies and their princess'
Call upon all the earth angels
Find the purest of hearts
To fill the boot, post a blog, sell a quilt, bake a cookie, hold a yard sale, hold a spaghetti supper, have an auction, raffle something nice, hold dances often, call in the clowns, go camping for fun, blow up the bounce houses, make-a-wish and it will come true.

Little Miss Felicia
Born April 4
Stolen from us by ignorance
Fear
Abuse
And love
Taken in the dark of the night

2.25.16

8:08 p.m. Felicia has come for a visit. She shows me a logging road. There is a chainsaw it works hard to cut down trees. After quite a while the saw stops. I hear one man clearly but do not know what he is saying. There is someone else. I believe it is a male. He is like her Dad. He is a little bit taller. His hair is darker. I get the creeps. This noise I hear that is like a chain saw. I feel like it is a snow sled. How she gets to where she is.

Felicia asks, "Take a ride with me". Once you get there is a walk but you can't get to it from the road you must walk.

Start at the store. I believe you go toward the river. I feel a pull toward the bridge. I feel it is on the right. How far I am not sure. I feel it is a road (maybe dirt road/trail/snow sled trail)

When I went to see Sgt. in Arms I got redirected to the same store 3 times. I couldn't believe it. I ended up going towards another town. I wanted to go further but needed to go home.

I feel it is on the right toward the river.

Smoker still comes up…. Pot

Co Ma

She shows me him and his mother. He is younger. He is a handful. He, I believe likes to steal. His mother can't help him. He is a mirror image of his father. Defiant and disrespectful to women.

What do the dates 1992/2000 mean…? I feel like there is a record of either misbehavior or maybe mom had trouble coping.

The month of April
The month of May

July keeps coming- Fireworks, ticker tape parade, red, white and blue, a cake for me. The star spangled banner.

Bounce houses

Anah Temple – No luck they only do hospital fund raisers….Sorry sweetie! WE will work it out. I promise.

What is the date 1993-2000 Dad?

The # 4 keeps coming up

She was drugged, there is smoke someone is high

Felicia is crying- Call mommie

Over the past four months Felicia keeps showing me her sitting at the kitchen table. I hear her crying. It tastes awful. She doesn't want it. Daddy keeps telling her "just eat it/drink it.

I feel it but can't see it……someone else is there!

I keep seeing the name Alex….Who is Alex?

Felicia keeps referring to Dad as TAZ- the Tasmanian devil???

Who has a Chevy truck/Chevy Silverado??? Black red??? Letters on the back wheel well area?? I feel like this truck is still being used. It has a loud muffler/ motor. It has an exhaust leak or I smell gas.

Cora draws a small picture in pencil----It is Felicia

She shows me 2 men dumped the body.

Disappeared 12.16.11

Map 76

Find Bacon St.

Railroad bed around the river, straight around, goes around and doesn't connect back to the original railroad bed. Right by the river off College Ave.

Gas station- video-paid with cash

Dirt road- next to highway, next to rive, snowmobile trail.

"So close yet so far away". Felicia

Cooler wrapped in plastic, cooler is locked, padlock.

Cliff, lily pads, East/West

There is a fence or rock wall

(I'm not sure??? May be nothing?? #_45-3870

Ethan??? Jaime???

Is there a well??? Empty??? Old??? Not very deep

A small amount of water

New/old bridge- (Railroad)

She was medicated/Tylenol/ibuprofen/lithium a cocktail-

Cora gets injection. I get she is forced to drink this.

Fighting/eating drinking it ("you better watch out you better not cry you better not pout I'm telling you why. Santa Claus is coming to town).

Who is Alex Again?

Train (R.R. Again)

Wharf/port

Poisoned

POW---prisoner of war Felicia and the children of Maine. Passing on the illness of abuse…..

She keeps showing me Julia Roberts…. This is my favorite actress??? Is it her mother's favorite??? Or just mine??

I love the lady in red…. Also this Princess Diana and the cardinal who I sing with for four days.

I hear the word FINE….. The little boy from Erin Brockovich. Attitude and a little shit….. This was Daddy when he was little and now He can't help it. He turned into his father.

2.27.16

1:41 a.m. Felicia's whisper from 'THE OTHER SIDE".

So many words come at me as she startles me awake again.

In the spirit world what does #4 mean?

In our world. His light workers 4/4 means her birthday. She wants a birthday party.

I wish for everyone to sit still and just listen. Hear her from the "OTHER SIDE'.

She is choreographing her own??? Documentary/movie??

She wants you to use Adele's 25 c.d. To touch all the lives from the outer circle. The places where we are too small to reach.

An example of a beautiful soul. From this side. A coincident or was it meant to be>

I know His plan was from long ago.

Felicia's whisper "FROM THE OTHER SIDE".

2.26.16
Felicia takes me there. I see Cedar Ridge??? Is this a real place?
There is a cedar tree to the right of this tree is a small pond of water-how deep I'm not sure. She is here!
Thank you honey.....

She gives me the words.... She shows me Ellen more than a few times.
The Shaw House
Sarah's House
The House that Jack Built
AYLA FAITH'S LEARNING CENTER

Cardinal X 4 this week
Princess Diana while I brush my teeth.... Plain as day in my face. I knew immediately that this is an Angel helping to make this Center come to life. She is doing her beautiful work from the other side still today through this tragedy!!! I want to cry.... My heart hurts and I know this is so big!!! I hope someone will listen.... Please!
I am floored at her appearance.
Again an angel with Golden wings.
A woman of pure love on both sides.
Felicia shows me books falling from Heaven
Falling for the children
Falling for the teachers
Nothing benefits one person---Souly
But, everyone gains wholly
A team effort must be had in order to achieve His plan.
Save His children
Start their
Start in Maine
Have Faith, work hard
Her love will spread like a wildfire.

"If you build them, they will come".
Schools, classrooms, values and love.
A center

AYLA FAITH'S CENTER a gift for all who need it.
She knows. Let her lead the way. A mother bear-brown. ME.
She can make it happen.
I know. That's why you hear me whisper "FROM THE OTHER SIDE".
Little Miss Felicia
(Heartbroken)
Mend it, well
Love!!

I wake @ 3:33 a.m.
A message from H.D. Barrett
A new center to pay it forward
You are given a gift today
See it no other way!
I see a sunflower-many sunflowers.
(Sign—yellow)
Today will bring for the many miracles.
Embrace them and TRUST HIM.
For now is the "HOUR".
To shine bright and show the world HIS gifts.
The light workers.
His little LIGHT.
Please let it shine.

A-waking
Coughing---- Sunflower- a mosquito- my Dad/a gift in his name, if you
will. Because of my love of him and all he is.
HE is risen: Books? Many books? Amy and the children for the last 25 years.

5.5.9 A date what is this date??????
He- 1ˢᵗ
Me-then you

Please change!!! Now is the time! Don't be too late…. Don't miss HIS message.
Change now for all of the world around the world.
Maine is 1ˢᵗ on the map.
I have been trying to figure out the # 9??
#9----Believe in HIM
Believe in AYLA FAITH AND LITTLE MISS FELICIA!!!
Is this so??? Do you or do you not love me?

Ayla Faith's Learning Center
I first get Bangor area…. She shows me a place in Dexter where Ayla Faith lives. It is beautiful. You have to see it to know what she sees for the potential!!!!!
This is a thank you too Bella's family for all your hard work over the eight months.

We need board members
Community
Committee
Fund Raising
Volunteers
Donations
Auction
Dances and fun. Love. Family
Required Children of all needs and backgrounds
Required curriculum- Planting and seeds, teach them to grow-food and love. Don't forget ME. Bring Him back to life. Keep her Faith.
Holistic health integrated for the Mind/Body/Spirit experience with self and wholeness.
Teach them how to take care of themselves without it being therapy- make it second nature
Teach them to accept one another
History/culture and religion (no one denomination)
No-One is right
No-one is wrong
Just have faith and believe
Core values only-no politics
Let that come as they develop their own values over the years.

Stronger minded
Stronger Faith
Stronger Maine
Stronger Nation
Stronger world
United we stand!
Spread it around.
Plant this seed of wellness.
Love/Faith/Forgiveness
From Felicia's BAND OF ANGELS...... hear them roar-fighter jets.

The Big one's FELICIA'S BAND OF ANGELS.......
God
Jesus Higher Powers that BE!
Mary

Apollo- SEE'R-Meditation
St. Bernadette-SEE'R-Meditation
St. Michael- For all
St. Raphael- For all+ more
PRINCESS DIANA
M. JACKSON
R. WILLIAMS
MARILYNN and the KENNEDY BROTHERS so many more.... Great
ones here and beyond.
My angels are Henriech Cornelius
Charles Fillmore
All of my earthly family
I say thank you to all of the Band of angels who have come together for
this amazing journey.
This is powerful stuff
Believe it or not!!!

2.28.16
Time doesn't matter
I will write my unending story

It started 10 years ago for me.
My first admission @ the mental facility

I see. I am a See'er.
Seer ship comes to me. A word that comes from the Bible. A word that I write down as I read the passages when I need inspiration.
I bare witness who will stand with me. Who will believe Little Miss Felicia?
It is time to walk the walk and talk the talk.
I work hard like the "mole".
I play little.
He remembers me standing before Him. I am only three years old.
I give my heart to Him that day.
2.25.16 this matters.
He asks me....... "HOW MUCH DO YOU LOVE ME"
He asks...... "HELP ME, RISE FROM MY KNEE'S.
A nation under God in despair.
Save His children.
Save our own children.
Start here!
This book!
Help me to reveal His true love.
Tell us what's inside this......
I will move your Heaven and Earth with one word.
LOVE
REMEMBER
ME
ONE
CHILD
AT
A
TIME
Fill in these blanks-Felicia, Nicole, Tavielle, Morgan-------------------,----------------------,---------------------,on and on and on.

Please sign this sheet....... Let's have a party in her memory. Raise some money for fun and love.

Start with a Princess Ball. Invite the fairies. And all the handsome Prince's in the land from far and wide. Raise money for the center and raise awareness for all of His children.

The 6th sense.

Please pass His test.

Reveal your own passion.

Carry, bare witness.

Feel His pain no more.

It is too much to carry alone.

He will rise again out of His own ashes.

To Felicia's mom from Chelsey

Arrows from my heart

I am on bended knee

I ask thee

Take these arrows from my heart

Too long have I wanted to see His Miracles?

Take these arrows from my heart

He kept His promise

Rainbows and ribbons

Tickets of love

Take these arrows from my heart

Walk with pride

Wear all the colors of her rainbow

Take these rainbows share them with the world

Hear her heart beating as you take these arrows

From my heart!

Don't just remember me!

Remember them all

The #4 = April 4th Felicia's birthday month and day.

The number of years she is missing

Happy birthday Honey!

Reborn- July 4th

Maine

Felicia loves Lilies. It doesn't need to be just Easter Lilies. She wants all kinds of colored lilies.

Felicia is the Bunny and the squirrel I see. She is quick and she gathers MY nuts. This is a process for me and she knows it. I am learning as I go and it is difficult. Spring will come and the flowers will bloom whether they find her or not.

She tells me and so does He. PROOF ME! We will find her. Just ask Bella and Courtney to lead the way! She wants to come home! For mommies and her family and then for the rest.

I have a vivid dream- My gift from God. Stephen. He was born a rough start. He is so good now. He is smart and so full of love and energy. A lesson for all of us. He is a mix of it all for me. My own rainbow wrapped in a bow straight from heaven. Meme loves her little hero. I love you to infinity and beyond.

Felicia says thanks to Bella and Courtney. Build the center and help your family and others like you.
Golden Wings
Her face appears everywhere I turn
Those eyes! Deep and dark filled with His love….
She receives her golden wings.
I am overwhelmed with His/her persistence
Still after all these years her beauty clings to me
Like the dew on the rose
My heart soars as she receives her golden wings
Up high above the clouds she spreads her wings….
Taking flight to spread His love to those below
Can you see hear?
Can you feel her?
Know that she is for filling her destiny!
She is the perfect likeness….
The perfect image! She is you!
Her Gift
My pencil flows freely
It is attached to my heart

My legs are weak
Like that of a new born fawn
She was His gift to the world…..
Even as this all turns into what seems like the end. It is just the beginning.
Little Miss Felicia has shown me much wisdom. Even through her pain.
Even though there is no way to take back what has been done.
"I LOVE YOU MOMMIE & DADDIE"
Equally as the day I was born. No matter what I will keep His promise.
Will you!
I love you all

Little Miss Felicia

2.26.16

"Mommy"…

In my third eye I see a small chain. Just the clasp remains. Is there a necklace somewhere?

I feel sad. Like a weight heavy around your neck.

I close my eyes and I can't erase those eyes. Her smile and those tiny teeth.

I want someone I don't know who. To help me draw or paint a photo/ painting of her. The scene I saw. A beautiful sight.

There was a purple/black sky as far as the eye could see. Stars were everywhere. But you were the biggest star. You seemed just a little bigger. Your hair was so old, like big girl you stood before me. A velvet gown of the deepest blue hue. It had long sleeves and a white lace trim collar. The ornament (Christmas 2009) my necklace- Please make it look like my ornament. I want it big to hang for all to see. She knows where, she knows who. Make my last wish a gift for you. The center.

A picture of me. In the Kingdom of God. Happy and loved. Make it one of a kind. Hang it for all the world to see. To remember me.

Moon babies: A school- for His special crystals, Indigos and the moon babies. Those who have trouble sitting. Boys and girls. Learn how to teach them. Use your hands to teach I beseech you. Don't use drugs to sit them in a chair. Use love to be kind and help me find my true color. Let me be me.

Labels of all kinds. None with a meaning.

When the day is done just hug them and love them no matter what. You never know when it will be your last.

Tuck them in tight. Leave the light on and don't ever forget they are a gift. A lesson to learn. He asks "did you learn"?

From Source
Our Lord God of Heaven and Earth

Give mommies a special gift from me. Fill up all you know will make her smile. In the end we will be together. Just for now hold onto these gifts. Pictures of me everywhere.

Take me for walks.

A box I prepared. Like a squirrel gathering nuts. It has "blue birds" on it. She sings it to me daily. "BLUE BIRD, BLUE BIRD ON MY SHOULDER". When you see the blue bird. It is her. Flying gracefully. Strong and wild. Like the eagle its wings will touch the world. Like God she keeps her promise. Remember me! I remember you!

I keep singing MOON RIVER! I think this is for Martha. My best friend. She moved. I miss her terribly. He says he was with you in Italy. He keeps showing me the flag. He says he sees you crying. Don't. It hurts to see you so sad. He shares the smell of almond butter with me. Your favorite nut. I remember this!

He is pure love. He is walking with the Man! He is pure love. You already knew that. I tested Cora's gifts. I thought of you, Charles. I thought of the man who stood by my side as I make the decision to stay or to go. My own near death experience. I of course stayed.

I asked Cora? Tell me about this person that I am thinking about.

He comes forward. Charles. He shows Cora he is handsome like my youngest boy Corey. A ladies man.

I try to get him to share with her how he died. He tells her "she doesn't need to see that". She has seen it brought to her so many times before.

2.28.16
Another sleepless night. I wake again 2:25 a.m. I am covered in sweat and my heart still won't stop pounding out of my chest.

I tell her "Felicia, I won't give up". I will fight until the end".

Your baby girl is as stubborn as they come. You make me smile, honey. My heart warms through.

My own babies keep me going. Keep me fighting for you.

Mary Ann, Billy and Corey Stephen-Meme's Hero. Cora and Ayla and not to mention Hayley and my new baby coming in May. I can't wait to meet you sweetie. Another miracle to come in the spring.

I send Mommy one more message straight from you!

Hear her!

Another sleepless night!

A Marriage Made In Heaven

3.1.16

4:34 a.m. I am given another piece of this puzzle. The deeper meaning behind His plan for me and a few of those I love.

He shares with me the symbolism of marriage. The piece of the puzzle for the meaning of my life, my sister Amy, Courtney-Ayla Faith and Little Miss Felicia.

Believe it or not. This is it. You choose.

He shows me time and time again. I am three years old and I stand before Him. An innocent child not even aware of the hell that lay ahead for myself. As I gaze into His eyes and I feel the love that flows from Him there is a bond that occurs. A marriage. My first marriage to our Savior- Our Lord our God.

His beauty is evident in all that He gives us. We just forget it. Lose it in our own ego. We forget to fear Him. We think we are better or stronger than Him. We forget to sit still and just listen to the words that He speaks. The words that he gives us. Our inner knowing. Our own intuition.

This I have learned from my own experience. A lesson my grandson had to pay. I didn't listen. I am at my mother's house and I am visiting with her as I try to give her His gift of my grandson. An important part of my life. An extension of me, through my daughter.

A miracle straight from God. His father bares witness to God's greatness. He gives the world many miracles. He is the father of many gifts. Many miracles straight from heaven. This is the only way he knows how to give. Through life. He shares His love with the world with the birth of his own children.

My daughter's boyfriend, my grandson's father. Samuel. Another gift from God. People I see judge him. No one judges him more than he does Himself. It took me a long time to see this. I am guilty, as the rest of the world. Mine eyes are open and I share with you in my sins of this tragic situation. ******* Point******

Amy's marriage- She stands in front of the world to protect herself and even me. The sapphire ring in my sketch book.

Princess Diana- Another beautiful sapphire ring with diamonds special to her and all have seen it.

The diamond heart shaped ring in my sketch book is for Felicia. Taken to young but not without a lesson. The one I set before you now.

The ring of fire. That is my journey with all of this. I am like an asteroid coming fast. Burning bright toward earth I fall. Will I crash and take the world by storm? Will I just fizzle out and it all be lost and for not? Please help me to PROOF HIM. He asks me from the other side.

I ask Him to proof her so I can prove HIM.

As I prepare for revealing Little Miss Felicia to the public's eye one more time. She teaches me sign language. She wants the children to learn sign language. I dance to Adele's song. It is the first song on her new c.d. 25 "from the other side". Felicia teaches me her own sign. Communication IN…. Communication OUT….. She teaches me giving this information up to HIM…. She teaches me the word sunshine/yellow…She teaches me Kiss me……..she teaches me please and thank you…. She teaches me I LOVE YOU.

Felicia wants me to learn how to give the children back their happy, their joy, and their love. The next song # 2 is a dance she wants. She shows me the colors of the rainbow and material. It is sheer and see through. The children use this "like" a ticker tape parade". On stage this is like the fairies are coming to life and seeing her in a magical way. The only way she can give you HER HAPPY, HER JOY, HER LOVE. From the "OTHER SIDE".

Felicia is orchestrating her own coming out party. Coming back. Giving back.

Felicia wants to share with the world the journey she has taken me on to bring her back. She wants me to share the things she has given to me to help proof her on the other side.

I have a room full waiting for MOMMIE. She wants Mommies joy, happy and love back…..She wants Trisha to have a sparkle in her eye again. This is the only way she feels she can make that happen. It is a process. It is a long journey and a painful one and she knows that. It must happen this way. Because it does not just affect one life. It affects so many. It has happened to so many. Taken away too young. Cruelly and like thieves in the night.

Share it with the world. Help them to heal. Help them to find me and help them to bring me home again. Happy Birthday to me. Happy Birthday to Mommie and Happy Birthday to the world.

Little Miss Felicia

Reborn-3.1.16

Hello my name is Bella Louise and I am a see'er, a light worker and a medium. I am co-founder of LOST SOUL SPIRIT CONNECTIONS.

Back in October of 2015 while my partner Cora and I were working our first case Little Miss Felicia came through to me. She gave us our signature name "The Scooby Doo Crew".

Over the past eight plus months Felicia has been communicating from the other side and has many messages for her mother.

The biggest message that Felicia wishes for Courtney and I to share is that she misses her mother and her family. She wants to let her community and the rescue efforts to return her home have touched her heart and she wants to send a special thank you to Sgt. in Arms for all of his dedication to her case.

In the past eight plus months Felicia has shown me and communicated much information. Most of it has to do with a special project that she has asked Courtney and me to do in celebration of her life.

She has helped me pick out special things to share with her mother all while communicating from the other side. I have a treasure chest of special gifts for you. I have a room full of ideas and dreams that she would love to share with her family and her community.

Little Miss Felicia would love to start with a special dance for her birthday celebration. She would love to see all of the Princess' and Fairies gather with their families. She has asked that special invitation be given to family and her close community first. She would love to have a few select songs that she has been singing with me over the past seven months. She has special colors that she wants at the dance. She wants a huge birthday cake for everyone to share.

Felicia tells me she wants LILY's for flowers. She wants colors of the rainbow to be brought to the dance. She wants this to be a special occasion to help raise money for a learning center.

She wants it to be called Ayla's Faith Learning Center. She has given Cora and me many ideas for raising money for this center.

Felicia has given many reasons why she would love to have this center and one is to bring faith and love back into her family's lives and in the community that has worked so hard for so long to bring her home.

Cora and I are reaching out to the community and to Felicia's family for support and help with this project. All that Felicia wants is going to take lots of hard work and lots of love to put it in motion. She realizes that in taking so long to get all of the information to us that we are probably not going to get everything done by her birthday. It is just too soon. Cora and I are shooting for by the end of May to have this first project to be underway.

We are putting together a committee for Miss Felicia's birthday bash. If there is anyone who is interested in volunteering to get this project off the ground and if you have any fund raising ideas please feel free to contact me @r Lost Soul Spirit Connection Facebook page Godstruthwillrise.

In regards to the room full of gifts for Felicia's mom I would love to share all that she has given me for you as she communicates from the other side. I hope you receive this message. I wasn't sure how else to get the support needed to get this project where Little Miss Felicia wants it to go…. To her center….

She wants to give a gift of her love back to the community and back to the state of Maine.

LOST SOUL SPIRIT CONNECTION has already received donations for an auction and we are collecting change for Felicia's project. When enough money is gathered I will open a special account especially for this project. She wants it to be known as Ayla's Band of Angel's project- For Ayla's Faith Learning Center. She has shared with me where she would like the first center located. She has shared with me a lot about the structure and basis for the center. In communicating with this little angel from the other side I have learned a lot about her own band of angels from the other side. She has many influential angels from the other side. She has shown me Princess Diana, Michael Jackson, The Kennedy brothers and many more. This is a huge project and Felicia knows I have the heart and dedication to pull this off. One day at a time and one fund raiser at a time. Thank you for any and all help with project.

LOST SOUL SPIRIT CONNECTIONS has also received important confidential information on her last hours with us. She has shared sensitive information back in late October to Early November and this information was shared with Police. Cora and I have waited along with Felicia to hear back from them but to no avail that has not occurred. Many weeks ago Little Miss

Felicia started communicating with more messages and information. She is not going to give up until her voice is heard.

I have contacted Police and they have informed me that the case has been transferred to the State Police. They are aware of Felicia's communications from the other side and has given Lost Soul Spirit Connections permission to search for her body based on our information given over the past several months.

The only thing I ask is for assistance in knowing where the searches have been conducted to help narrow down this information that Felicia has given Courtney and I in great detail. We have solved one other case and helped in putting one woman's tragedy put to rest. I hope the community can back us up to get the help to put Felicia's wishes in action and help to remember her with love and dignity only.

Little Miss Felicia's book of great detail is being written and this book will help raise money as well for Ayla's Faith Learning Center. Names have been changed. This is Felicia's wish and I will make sure her voice is heard one way or another. Lost Soul Spirit Connections hopes for any and all help in getting Little Miss Felicia's voice heard from the other side and getting her project off the ground. Thank you to all who will help, God blesses you and so does Little Miss Felicia.

Ghost Writers From The Sky

2/27/16

It's been a busy day. Not much sleep again last night. I hope your script works. I pray and I know it will. I must keep FAITH. If I don't this will be all for not.

After all of today's information and let downs and songs from above and all of their love, I still try to sleep. Felicia jolts me from a sound sleep. I have only been laying down for about thirty minutes. Sleep comes easily to me now, I just can't stay asleep. Different from any other time.

My heart pounds out of my chest and my head feels like it will come off my shoulders at any minute. I realize that this is when Felicia comes to me in my dreams. She shows me what she wants and then I jump, back into this world. She is showing me her Christmas wish list.

She has chosen a select few. Angels in the sky. Ghost writers from the other side. I don't know where to start. The beginning of the list or the end.

In a revelation this morning getting ready for what was supposed to be the biggest moment in history, well it didn't happen. Why, because he is teaching us as we go along. Trust up and keep FAITH. He is still in control and it will unfold in the best interest of all.

So, I am excited, nervous and the butterflies are bouncing in my stomach as I gather all of her gifts for her mom. I feel like a whirlwind, preparing HIS last supper. A feast for all to witness. I give all of the gifts that she and I have gathered over the past four months. Ribbons and bows. Books galore. Glue and glitter. Fairies and butterflies. A great big box especially for MOMMIE! I love you. Can you tell?

A GOD box is so special a connection beyond comprehension. WE went for walks in the nature and Felicia shows me only what she wants me to keep. I have red berries and pine cones. Rocks shaped like hearts. A special fern of green in the depths of winter. She shares with me "this is my giggle". Sent straight from Heaven. A gift you can remember it came with you. I see and gather milk weed from the fields around. A strip of bark from His place on HIGH. Take mommy there and show her where I am. The place I chose until she could be there. Don't be sad when you look at these gifts for they are all for just you. My birthday gift to YOU!

I have gathered me a band. A music entourage. They come from very high. The band is called "Felicia's band of angels. They help me to sing and dance and remember the good. For out of all these ashes that is all that we should.

Felicia and I sing with the cardinal birds all week. The red feathers are such an eye catching sight next to the white.

As I brush my teeth she shows me a sight. My heart aches and I am in disbelief. A flash of an earth angel. Transcended too young. It explains to me now why. Why the overwhelming preparation and the tailoring of such a grand coming. 'PRINCESS DIANA". A soul of God's pure love. She helps with this because the healing is in desperate need. To show a nation in ruins. To come back to life. A hope is renewed for young and for old.

The schools have lost their values. The kids have lost their hopes. Parents have forgotten what is important.

The preparation for this "PRINCESS & FAIRY BALL" is just the beginning. To change. Helping all of those who are still to come. Children that have no hope without HIS love.

The wheels are set in motion. Plans are in the works. It is time to dig in let's get ready to work.

There are to be dances and many. Let family be the core value that shines through this tragedy. Awareness is the key. Let's stop this madness. Before it's too late. The world around us is falling fast. Into a black abyss. Too much hate, too much judgement. Not enough love and faith.

"AYLA'S FAITH LEARNING CENTER" a great place to begin. Her band of angels will help orchestrate this GRAND OPENING. When and where is still unknown. She is confident that with faith and love it can all be done. Thank you again Miss Felicia…. What a beautiful gift to give to the world!!!

Felicia shares with me a song. Over and over and over. Adele's #1 song from her new c.d. From the other side. WE sing this together for many months as I prepare to make my faith in her and Jesus known.

This song helps to revive my spirit and faith in all that we at LOST SOUL SPIRIT CONNECTION have worked so hard for in the past several months. Courtney and I have lived breathed and will die trying to get this message to Felicia's mom.

Some people may believe it to be more than just what it is. A cry from the other side. A plea to hear her voice. Nothing more. A tiny voice taken away way too soon. Tragedy and sickness weaved from the same cloth. Felicia asks us all to take notice of her senseless death. She shares her knowledge of the connection between the abuse of his childhood being the only misunderstood link to her disappearance and death of a child taken too soon.

Will any of this bring her back? NO. Will any of this ease the pain of her loss? No.

It will only give us hope to change the future of the world. One child at a time. One person at a time and one community can lead to a greater nation. One, under God. Just like it used to be. The great values handed down from generations ago.

As I listen to the song "From the other side". Felicia tries to teach me sign language. Some of it is real sign language. Some of it is her own signs.

She shows me communication sign. She shows me connection sign. She shows me the sign for yellow. Umbrella. She shows me please. I love you. And she shows me Thank you.

She was very young when she went to be with Jesus. He has her surrounded by her own band of angels. Special angels. Angels full of love. Angels full of song. Angels full of goodness and purity. My drawings that go along with my dreams and third eye visions will help to give a visual into Felicia's connections from the other side. Everyone open to this are invited to buy the book that she wants written. A book to help build the learning center that she wants built to help those children in most need. Those children who can't sit still and learn.

November 4, 2015

Dear Puppa,

This is the rest of the Spirit Connections that I have had with Felicia. It has been edited for ease of understanding. Felicia is stuck as I mentioned in my last e-mail I have scheduled a meeting to help her transition.

I hope as a mother and grandmother that you will give mom a chance to decide for herself if she would like to be part of this transition for Felicia. I know in my heart this could be a very healing process for her. I would also like to invite 1 or 2 more people to witness this process from the immediate family.

I have this scheduled for November 16, 2015 @ 1:00p.m. If you talk to Felicia's mom and decide that you would like to join us I would need a little notice to prepare the way that Felicia has shared with me how she would like it.

You can contact me by phone or by e-mail. I hope to hear from you and have a blessed day.

Bella Louise Allen

November 2, 2015

Felicia is still with me throughout the day today as I clean. She is persistent in getting through to me and to her family. God bless you sweetie.

In the crib I see a stuffed elephant with spots. The elephant has weighted down feet. The words remember me come to me.

When I vacuum I pull the crib out and underneath the crib is another elephant- (This elephant and the one in the crib represent Felicia). This elephant has a blue blankie, it reminds me of a child that may have sucked her thumb and held the blankie at the same time. (Did Felicia do this?).

There is a naked doll, white cloth stuffed with a life like head, no hair. The eyes on this doll are amazing blue. They seem to pierce right through your heart. There is a velvet blue blankie under her.

The black lab puppy shows up again 3 times. I believe the black lab puppy's represent the cops looking for Felicia

Did someone get a black lab puppy? If so when???

I still see Christmas/Santa Claus. It comes to me the case may be reopened before Christmas.

Is there any one associated with a Campground?
Evergreens???? Trees
I see a tipped over well made of rocks- I believe this to be the healing that will occur with her transition.

That's all so far today. It's in God's hands Felicia, you're doing such a great job for such a little Angel!

November 3, 2015
I ask my ascended masters and master guides for help with any information that I am missing or information that Felicia may be holding back.
At 6:22 I wake
I know the words: Smoky, green, fog
More puzzle pieces
November 3, 2015
Again Felicia is with me on and off throughout the day.
She is still trying to tell me where she is. After much information is put before me, I have to sit back and put the puzzle pieces together. I am new to this and I learn at the speed of lightening to help Felicia get her wish.
I had an appointment with Candace today. I tell her most of everything I know about Felicia and I find out from Candace that she is STUCK!
Felicia needs help and I can either help her move on or I can invite her family to see her where she is and they can heal and help their little angel to move on.
I sent an e-mail to Puppa and I wait for his response. I trust in Jesus and so does Felicia that he still has faith, even just a little or he wouldn't still be trying so hard to do all that he does.

Being psychic doesn't mean 100% right all the time. It can be like bits and pieces of information.
Felicia being so young her energy is quick as lightening and it can sometimes be hard to catch every detail that she is giving us.

This work can be very rewarding for the loved ones who are at a loss so great they can't seem to move one foot in front of the other.

In doing this work my only goal is to give some kind of peace or closure to the lost souls of all involved.

Lost Souls Spirit Connection
May you feel peace and love from His white light!
God Bless

November 5, 2015
Father- alcohol/drugs past abuse circumstances/life makes people make horrible choices.
The ones they love the most end up hurt
Girlfriend/sister and especially Mothers will help to protect until the end

Felicia fears for others- other children he has contact with or his own to be born

729 Lakeview Drive South China, Maine
Lily Pads from earlier entry….. There are dead lily's going along the front or side of the barn shaped house. There is a slab under the red painted wood barn shaped house with 2 white garage doors. Left door is up (I see something blue on the floor) (possible sign of the blanket Felicia is wrapped in) the right side door is down. There is one window on that same wall as the garage doors, then an entry door.

The side I face has 2 windows down below. I can only focus on the one window above. The top part of the wood is left natural or with a shine to it- polyurethane?

I have seen for 5 days sewer, drain, or well????

I see through the window--- the shape of an angel!!!
The roof has sheet metal covering it. I see mostly green, but at times it looks like it is blue.

Beside the red barn is the back end of a bright red truck with 4x4 on the back fender

There is a corn field on the backside of the barn

I see a road with like a small island in the middle. I see a pine tree white and green sign beside the road closest to the barn.

E/W I think is being mistaken for this road with a small island in the middle of it.

The New Hampshire I believe Felicia is referencing about is me. I am a new hamster----chasing my tail on a big round wheel!!!

92- I think is being transposed.

1807 Pond Meeting House (friend's camp)????

There is a white building like a town hall or "Meeting House".

???????? Of apple tree?????

One last link??????Sexual abuse?????????? I won't go into details here.

November 6, 2015

I get pork pie with Mom…. Dad is a pig, treats women as if they are nothing.

The body found in 2004, does he have a connection at all with the town of South China or the barn house or family that lived/live there?

I am getting he is the man at the mobile station- Name S. He bought a candy bar and bought gas????

I get a coffee cup

(Wake up and smell the coffee or heat it up and don't forget the donuts)

Reopen the case

A vase

(Flower's to remember her by/put her to rest)

A water bottle (tears are falling after all this time)

A magnetic refrigerator (keep coming up empty-cold case)

Dog eared photo's (cops are tired)

T-shirt now worn and faded all with beaming blond hair-(explains itself

The family and the community will never forget

I get this to mean I know you're tired but please remember me
Don't give up hope
I trust you Sgt. in Arms please don't give up on me

I see new sneakers untied
Stars
Don't miss this opportunity
Dig- I have seen repeatedly

I get the blue that she is wrapped in a blanket or a bathroom rug

So close yet so far!!!

Red, green, blue, yellow circle!
Then a Red, green, blue, white circle!

2:43 a.m.
3 spinning, floating white lotus on a pond (I hear the word locust at the same time)
They all know everything
They all are dying inside
They all feel guilt

Crystal Clear

2.17.2016

Cleaning house has just begun. Putting myself first is my goal. I am that I am and I may fail. I know I can pick myself up by the boot straps and start new. I have done it a thousand times and I will continue to until the end of time.

I started my new journey today. I thank God daily now for all of His love. I sing Happy Birthday every day. It is like I am born anew with each sunrise. I wake with anticipation of what the day will bring.

My biggest challenge will be my gift of love. I have always wanted to please others. Their needs would come before mine. I know that after forty-eight years I can no longer live a healthy life this way. So, call it being selfish, self-centered or egotistical I will come first so I can free my heart to help others in their journey.

In my quest for self-love I received a wonderful gift from a great woman I don't even know. I received a pay it forward gift from Katie and Kevin from The Holistic Center. This was given to Katie and Kevin after getting to know someone through Christ. Miracles that we don't even see occur through those that we meet and even those that we don't. I thank you to all who have helped me along the way on my journey. Praise be to God.

I was greeted at the Holistic Healing Center by Kevin. A soul of great spiritual being. We had an instant connection from the first time we met. He is my connection to mother earth. We had an opportunity to talk and he shared with me that he has been reading my first book "MIRACLES AMONG CHAOS".

I am grateful and will continue to be grateful for all that He sets before. My first book is only the lessons learned in this lifetime. I was blessed with many challenges and I believe I faced them with as much grace as I possibly could.

MIRACLES AMONG CHAOS- to me is not about the abuse that one suffers growing up in a dysfunctional family but about the love that we share when we finally figure out what we are here for. In order to find that love within our structure we must be able to forgive.

We can only forgive others after we see them through healed eyes. In my experience I wasn't able to give the forgiveness that my family needed and deserved until I forgave myself for all the failings that I felt I had done to them.

It is never an easy thing. Forgiving oneself. We must look deep in the mirror and find out who we truly are. It can take years but it can be done.

I had my first session with Katie at THE HOLISTIC HEALING CENTER today. I can't tell you how blessed I feel to have met Katie and Kevin. Ever since I have met them the fire inside of me that started when I was only three years old has been rekindled and I know in my heart there is no turning back. I am in it for the long haul.

I will have many choices to make in order to become the best me that I can be. I know I will not always make the best choices because I am after all only human. I forgive myself for that. Let the healing begin!

THROUGH THE LOOKING GLASS

My feet struggle daily to make that next step. Fear continues to pop its head up from the depths of these dark holes within my soul. I stand before this ugly mirror waiting patiently for its reflection to change. I only see the wrinkles forming and the silver touches of age to my temples. Will I work fast enough or stay on the straight and narrow long enough?

Are there truly angels in disguise walking among us? I believe each and every one of us truly is an "Earth Angel". We walk around and we perform miracles and we share His love. It may only be to hold the door open for a stranger or to pick up a dropped pencil but I have seen it in much bigger forms.

Paying it forward is only the beginning. It doesn't take much effort to show Him we remember His love for us.

Olivia

3/6/16

I am at work and I have been trying to get a grips on all that has come through. I still struggle with myself. Am I doing the right thing? I know in my heart of hearts I am. I am only one woman with one huge heart and that has to stand for something.

I spent the day with my grandson and had the time of my life. As I take care of my clients and visit with the biggest miracle that has ever happened to me, I see another lost soul.

Olivia comes to me. I see her holding hands with Felicia. There doesn't appear to be much difference in their ages. Olivia is a beautiful girl. She appears to be about 9-13 years old. She has long brown hair. It is wavy and thick. It goes down past her shoulders and it is coming out to the side on one side. She has light to medium brown eyes. I only see black and white leggings. I am not sure why she shows me these. I am only given her name and her beautiful face and then the black and white leggings.

As I think back over the past couple of days there has been additional information that has come in and I thought it was information for Felicia's case. I think this may be a run over from Olivia. I have confirmation of this… Ringing in my right ear!

I was finding myself confused because of the new information and now it makes sense. In seer ship, mediumship and physic abilities more than one spirit can come in at the same time. I believe this to be the case for some of the information on the Screwdriver. I'm not 100% sure of the why, with the screw driver. I feel sick and I have pains with this scene. Too painful to want to go there.

So I have met yet another child who is in need of assistance finding peace from the other side. How do I have a conscience and just let this go.

The top of my head hurts and I know it is a sign….. I can't let it go…. It won't let me go…. I will help Felicia and I will try my best in helping Olivia….

Be patient girls with God's love and guidance we can get the help we need. Peace to you both and hold tight to one another….

Meditation

6/7/16

Another day almost gone and I have been as busy as a beaver. I am at work and my clients are in program. I put the finishing touches on Ayla Faith's Learning Center. The plans for the summer are coming together. I put them down on paper so that I can be accountable for the things that I am given from the heavens above.

I make a list and I check it twice. I go to the print shop for the proofs of the T-shirt order information. I will give a copy to the local news media if they are interested. The local tv channel has received my package. I follow up with a call to another media out reach. I give the secretary the dates for a proposed interview date. June 13-16 are good days for me. I will wait and see who steps forward to hear Felicia's voice from the other side. Who will help me to get the attention she deserves. Who will help to get her center started? Who will help to get the yard sale planned, the T-shirts sold, the wrist bracelets on the wrists of all who will remember Felicia's faith and all of the missing and exploited children of Maine.

As I try to center and reboot with energy for this long haul ahead of me, I meditate. I use my stones amethyst, rose quartz and clear crystal quartz. I place the amethyst stone on my forehead, the rose in my left hand and clear crystal in my right hand. I center myself and breathe in Gods white light.

Jesus comes first. I know that St. Germaine is here. He stretches out His arms and he hugs me. Again he says I work too hard. It doesn't have to be this hard. If I just trusted in Him a little more. It will all come together. Stop chasing my tail and breath. I remind Him, "You know me better than anyone". "If you didn't want me to work so hard you should have chosen someone else". I smile and He knows I will do anything that He asks and it will be done.

I hear her in the distance. She comes and I sit with her. Jesus has gone. Princess Diana comes to me. We sit and I feel the warmth of her love. She smiles and her eyes sparkle with His love. She is proud of my hard work and my determination. She knows my heart as He does and she thanks me for a job this big will take many to pull it off. She tells me to be patient and to listen to all of the guidance that is available to me. I have a large number of Master-Teachers, Saints, and several bands of angels available to assist me. All I have to do is stop and ask whatever I need and I shall be given the guidance to do bring this learning center to the children that need it most. Princess Diana shows me a ring. The ring I saw in my vivid dreams. It is beautiful. I see the huge sapphire center. It is not round but almost a square shape. The sapphire is surrounded in crystal clear diamonds. There are so many diamonds. The deep blue of the sapphire reminds me of Little Miss Felicia's beautiful blue eyes. Electric blue and no one will ever forget those eyes as her face is embedded in the memory of some many who grew to love her through her own tragedy.

This beautiful ring means so much to Princess Diana. Someone special and dear to her heart. She shares with me the sadness that He felt for taking her when He did. Another lesson for all of those left to feel a deep loss and His blessings in our lessons are tested again. Through the loss of another earth angel…. Princess Diana shows me the tunnel and her last moments. Her heart was happy and she shows me her laugh. It was infectious to all who heard it. The reason he fell in love with her at such a young age. Yes, she shares with me Prince Charles and the love they once had for one another.

Princess Diana leaves and she and Felicia join and Jesus who waits in the distance near the willow tree that I see so often in my 3rd eye.

I again am humbled and I feel so much love and I know I must be patient and wait. For Gods plan will come to fruition in His time and no one else's. Praise be to God!

May 29, 2016

A poem for Little Miss Felicia and her angels…..

THROUGH THE LOOKING GLASS
I STAND ALONE LOOKING THROUGH THE GLASS
A PAIN TOO SHARP COMES, MY HEART ACHES
The thought of letting you go

I think of our trip to the Mountain
Mt. Hope Cemetery. I feel your peace
I feel the warmth of His son
How can I release you yet again?

Being passionate has brought me here
Being me has brought me to let you go
Fly Little Miss Felicia…..
Fly baby girl
Meme loves you to infinity and beyond.

Plant flowers in my memory. Plan my princess party. Bring fun to those who are still living my pain. Help them to remember what your wish is Meme! Peace & Love. Above all…. LOVE!!!

Princess party to benefit Ayla Bell's Faith Learning Center.

Cora & Ayla Faith- guests

Meme and anyone who wishes to come and remember me and all of the missing and exploited children of Maine.

Invite all the Princess' and Prince's that want to come. No limits

Scott- For Ayla Faith…His mom and Grandmother wishes him to see a miracle in the making. The Learning Center coming to life. Remember "Scotty can help you with that".

6/4/2016

Felicia wakes me yet again at 4:11. "A call for help Meme". Felicia is here. "I know he will listen". "Puppa".

Grace wins- Is the song her angels sing to me this morning. A beautiful song indeed.

I tell Felicia "I sent your message again honey. I will be patient. You know I'm not any better at it than you. We must keep faith in Him or how do we expect this miracle to happen. Bringing you & mommie together is our goal. One way or another. Through the learning center is our first step. Pray sweetie. Ask Him to help guide Puppa or Mommie to your website to see the post. I love you honey to infinite and beyond.

6/8/16

A walk to clear the cob webs. It's been a couple of days since my last walk. That doesn't mean that Felicia and her band of angels haven't been present. I just seem to connect better with the angels during sleep time and when I clear my head. It is more organized and less confusing. It becomes clear. The messages that Felicia tries to give me. Her band of angels are many and I am blessed to have communicated with them through Little Miss Felicia. What an amazing experience and I- not in a million years would have thought this possible.

He knows I am near the end of my ropes. I am frustrated and feeling very lonely. Although I am surrounded by so many angels. I walk to clear my head and I am greeted by my mourning dove. It is 6:10 a.m. He sits still and I think he is asleep. He jumps me, as he flies away. I walk by him just ten feet away, I see white tipped feathers and his back is now blue. My mourning dove shape shifts into a blue jay. The second time I have witnessed this. God is good and nature is truly amazing.

I walk and it is windy and I sense her presence. Little Miss Felicia joins me for my walk. She takes my hand. Hers is so small. Bigger than my grandsons but small just the same. Her fingers are warm and I can't see them but I can feel them. She asks me, "Do you like my dress"? It is the same one she wore a few days ago. A sundress. The dress she wore when she had her daisy entwined halo. An angel in the truest form.

I am quiet today and Felicia senses it. We walk and it is windy and I feel a chill deep in my heart. I am mad at God. I hate it when I have such feelings towards Him. I know part of this is a test for me. How far am I willing to go? He whispers over and over again. "How much do you love me"? I know He knows how much I love Him. I came back didn't I? I was at Heavens door and I chose to come back. For a while now I have known that this little project is more than just connecting Felicia with her Mom. I believe with all of my heart I came back for much more. All of my writing and journaling, dreamtime and meditation are just the beginning. My work book in progress I hope to shed some light on all of God's love and wonders. I hope to shed a little light on the labeling of mental illness. More than anything I want to bring Little Miss Felicia home to her mother and her family.

He asked me "Proof me".... I am trying my best and I feel like I am close to giving up. I have so many plans outlined and events to bring together and I reach out now several times a day to the public. I ask for help from God and the angels and I wait and I fear all these months my hard work and my tears will all be for nothing. I am trying my best to keep His faith, to hold His light but I feel it is getting dim.

I received the estimate for the t-shirts today. I want so badly to just order them and sell each one of them on the streets and sell my soul to bring this child home. I want to bring her home tomorrow, but that is not His plan. He shows me it must be done with love and grace. The process is not one that can be done overnight. I hold my head up high and I squeeze Felicia's hand and we walk. Mostly in silence. She knows I am struggling. She feels my anxiousness, she senses the tears I try to keep back as we look at the dark clouds that are rolling in. On our way back home I hear a dozen birds or more to my left and I look over. I don't see any birds but I see daisies and Felicia pulls me toward the other side of the road. I grin and I am reminded of her halo a few days ago. I go down the edge of the road into the tall grass and I pick 3 daisies. One for Felicia, one for mom and one for dad. She never forgets her dad. She knows more than she should. How to love even through such a difficult time as this. So young yet such a wise little angel.

We head back home and I almost trip over a small rock. She wants me to pick it up. It isn't any great shape or size it's the color that she likes. It is almost a reddish purple color. It is broken in half and I tell her I will put it in our box. Our special God box. It is blue and white and has mirrors on the sides. It is lined with black velvet. A beautiful box to put all of our nature treasures in. As we walk home the smell of Lily's is so over powering. I wonder why. There are no lily's anywhere. Just fields of hay that need to be cut. Buttercups, daisies and tall grass everywhere. Last time we walked the smell of lilies where present. In the same area too. Felicia showed me Lilies on our first days together. It makes me wonder if there is maybe a Lily in her life that she is telling me about. Is it just a flower that she loves or is it God sharing with me Easter! His resurrection??? I don't know. Only time will tell. As I walk, almost home now. She is gone. As fast as she came. She is just gone. No goodbye, just gone. I take a deep breath in and I thank her for her visit.

6/9/16

What a blessed day! After a short but restful night I got a lot accomplished and feel like things are going well. I picked up the flyers for t-shirt sales and information on the bottle drive and yard sale. I delivered these flyers to Katie. She wasn't at work so I left them with the secretary. I then went to the radio station and talked in length with the receptionist there about Ayla Faith's Learning Center and the upcoming fund raisers.

I then went to my beacon of hope. I met the receptionist there and talked in length about the project for the learning center. She explained to me about the process and that she would give all of my information to the man in charge. She said where it is a non-profit project that they would put the fundraisers on their events calendar. After going into detail about Felicia's communication and all that I am hoping to accomplish with this project the receptionist said that the man in charge may be interested in a 15 minute on air interview. I hope this happens. I hope they include this special project on their events calendar. I hope to get some committee members through this advertising and I hope to find a place to hold the yard sale in July. I hope to get enough money to get the t-shirts for sales and I hope to get the wrist bands for sales. I hope to get the community involved in the Ayla Faith's Learning Center and I hope to raise the roof for the children in need of a special, safe place to learn old fashioned values and to implement prayer and share God's love with special needs children from all backgrounds. Please, Jesus…..Mother Mary and all that is Holy to help. This project needs a miracle. God is great!!!!! I will wait for His miracle…..

As I arrive at work. I unload my car for my cleaning job and I see her under the pine tree. Princess Dianna, she stands graceful and her face almost glows as a smile crosses her lips. She glances my way and her hand comes up and she waves. Graceful and full of His love. She approves of the work that I have just done. Spreading His love and His light is an honor and I hope to do all that I can to "PROVE HIM". As I turn to go in I smell it. The lilies…. Princess Diana is my lilies. Her smell. When I can't see her. I smell her. She is the white calla lilies. She stands tall and strong and she is graceful in all she does and is. God's true light and love. An earth angel taken too soon and her love lives on through this project and Little Miss Felicia and all of her band of angels. Messages from the other side to a mother in so much pain. Waiting to bring justice to her baby girl.

Sacrificial Lambs

June 18, 2016

The sun is rising and I feel the heat coming through the window beside my bed. I hear the cardinal that visits me at work out my window. A lesson of love. A blessing in disguise is revealed as I meditate before starting my day.

A morning of self-love and self-care. I meditate to connect and get guidance on the day ahead. I center myself and ask for guidance from God, Jesus, Mary and all my Master Teachers and all of my special angels.

As I lay down I immediately am joined by Usui Sensei. I see him and I know he has been with me so many times. As I use his special healing gift. The gift of Reiki healing. I feel his love and his healing on a level like no other healing I have experienced before.

I stand at the top of the stairs in a mist, a fog of white beauty. I reach to the rail and I feel my way down the stairs. I can't see the steps yet I know I need to go. I need to share my lessons of faith, love and beauty. For all those who will open their hearts to God's love.

I make choices on my journey. Is it the past or is it the future that I visit? It is both.

Jesus walks to my right. He has my hand in His. Mother Mary is to the left. She holds my arm in hers.

As we walk in silence on this journey, the hall narrows and we become one. I am Jesus and I am Mary!

There is no door. The gate is not present. Heaven's door is open to all of God's children.

A choice is presented. Who chooses to believe? Who chooses to love? Who chooses to have faith?

I walk and I see Chelsey. My best friend's daughter who passed in a tragic accident over 10 years ago. Chelsey sits on a bench swing and one leg is up. Her chin is resting lightly on her knee. Her other leg drapes over the edge of the swing. She swings back and forth. She has a dress on. A light crème colored dress. Her beautiful dark hair is flowing in the breeze as she swings softly back and forth.

She doesn't see me. She is content and she is deep in thought. A slight smile is on her lips. I do not need to wonder what she is thinking about. My heart tells me. I know she is watching over her mother. Proud of how strong Carol has been through all of her lessons. Life has been hard for Carol and God loves her for her unending faith and love she has in His plan.

To the right of Chelsey I see Abby. Another earth angel taken too soon. Tragedy comes in waves and healing is in need for all of God's children. Abby is playing. She is surrounded by children. Young children surround her and they play and run. I hear squeals and giggles. They come from numerous little angels that are so happy in Heaven.

I feel a pull to the left and I walk. I am in awe of all the beauty I see. As I approach the river bank there is a rock. It is huge almost as big as I am. Round and it sits up tall. There is a red glow and it appears to be on fire and as I almost see the fire vividly it turns into a mist and cloud.

I realize what it is. I realize who it is….. God's presence is felt. A huge bold thing to say, to write, to know. I believe and He knows my love is unending and He knows I fear not who believes me.

He draws my eyes to the water. There is a basket. A baby lays quietly in the basket. I know who this baby is. Moses.

I sing over the past few months…. "Set my people free".

Moses has been with me and I felt it and now it is confirmed.

I learn passages from the Bible. I am directed in a way that you could only be directed for pure miracles to happen.

I take you back to the river. Baby Moses is wrapped in his cloth.

The basket that Moses is in changes to a green large elephant ear leaf. Moses turns into "Little Miss Felicia".

Sacrificial lamb comes to me. The words and then the meaning behind Moses and Little Miss Felicia.

Moses' mother sacrificed her son. She gave him up. She sent him in a basket to be with a queen who wished for a child. She let her son go in order to save his life.

I am given…. Felicia is taken from this world in order to save her from a life of terrible abuse. A sickness that was unavoidable due to ignorance and pain.

God is good. He gives us great things. He takes away for reasons that so many of us question. Why? Why me? Why you? Why her? Why him?

Stop questioning His love and just have faith it is for a purpose bigger and better.

Work past the pain. Remember His sacrifice. Remember Mary's sacrifice.

We are all sacrificial in one way or another. We are all lambs of God.

A blessing in a lesson. Felicia's passing. For so many to see. For so many to feel. The pain is great. As is all loses of God's children. Felicia's loss touches so many. An earth angel taken too young out of love.

God shows me and shares with me just one lesson. One blessing. He ends Felicia's suffering at the hands of her father to teach us love, faith and forgiveness.

As I come back he shows me the hallway. I know what He showed me and why. I am standing with Jesus and Mary again. Beside me.

Jesus places His hands on my head. Like I see the priest do to the small children. A gesture of love, a gesture of blessing, a gesture of thanks. He says thank you for your sacrifices.

Mother Mary holds my hands. She smiles and I know she will be with me through this journey. I am a chosen one. Like all of God's children. To teach, to love and to learn.

I am given a record. A black record. A vinyl record. He asks me to record my journey with Him. To share His love and His lessons. Share with others for hope. Share with others for Faith.

He reminds me…. "Prove me". "I will prove you".

"Let go"! "Trust up".

God is good. I see Robins everywhere. As I head back up the stairs robins circle me. Joined by the blue jay. I hear Him in the distance. An Eagle. My connection from so many years ago.

I am given a reading from the Bible….Ecclesiastes or the preacher

The book of man "under the sun" reasoning about life. Chapter 6

A visit to the astral planes

May 29, 2016 11:06 p.m.

I beg Him to show me the way!

I ask Charles, my best friend's husband who waited with me when I experienced my near death experience. I was given a choice to be by Jesus' side or to come back to finish my journey. I ask Charles ....

"What am I"?

He replies with no words. Just his thoughts. "You are love". "Pure and white"

I tell him "I am not worthy". "I feel so weak".

Charles replies. "You were worthy then and you are worthy now".

A song keeps coming…... I hear the melody but I can't put words to it.

I feel them all around me. The angels. High and low. Saints and earth angels I knew and lost.

I hear the birds singing on high. I hear the angels sing with them.

"True beauty and nothing more than love that is why". God whispers words of His love in my ear.

"You are strong". "You are your mother's daughter"…... "Daddy"!

"I love you". "I miss you". <3

My emotions take over and St. Germain comes to me. "Soon, it will all be revealed soon".

My reality starts to pull me back. I try to stay. I need to accept it. A chosen one for a reason.

My heart has been heavy for so long. Filled with so much pain.

I wasn't supposed to come back. I was supposed to fly with the angels.

I chose life before death. To help one more child besides my own.

"Little Miss Felicia"…... "Meme loves you honey"!

He tells me it's going to happen.

"Just hold on honey". He promises me He won't let me down. Not this time. I have been so good. So strong, through so much.

Mother Mary comes to me. She wraps me in her arms and I cry.......
Tears flow. Tears from exhaustion and tears from fear and I surrender.
I come back I couldn't stand it. To see such beauty and still have fear.
Who will ever believe it?
If I can't believe it and I have lived it.
Who indeed!!!
God does and that is all that matters. No matter what.....
He has always had faith in me.
He has always had faith in Felicia.
He has always had faith in Ayla Faith.
He has always had faith in Courtney.
Connections.....
Hope.......
Faith......
And above all LOVE!!!!!

A Marriage Made in Heaven

He shows me over and over again over the past eight months. Me standing in front of Him at the age of three. I am back at LaGrange Baptist church. He shows me giving my heart to Him. A love unending.

He asks me...

"What do you want"?

I struggle with this. I love to give. I hate to receive.

I tell Him "I want a ring". "A big shiny ring".

"I want lots of flowers on my birthday".

"I want an education to be able to have one job".

"I want to go to the movies".

"I want to sing under the stars".

"I want to go for a four-wheeler ride with Seth".

"I want to see my kids be happy".

"I want to see them be safe".

"I want to be loved by Seth without fear or judgement of loving my own children".

"I want a hair dye job".

"I want a new pair of shoes".

"I want my computer back".

"I want to print my books and share her story".

"I want to finish my book, into the fires of hell".

"I want to teach children to be the best they can be".

"I want to dress up and dance with all the Little Miss Felicia's of the world".

"I want her birthday party".

"I want her wishes to all come true".

"I want Khloe there". "I want her dreams to come true".

"I want Ann Marie's prince charming to just BE". "To love her for her"!

"I want Sam to love himself enough to know he's messing things up".

"I want Stephen to not have to sit in a chair drugged up".

"I want everyone to see how beautiful he is……

"So, smart….So handsome….His damn eyes".

"My HERO reminds me of LOVE".

"He reminds me of a song I want to write".

"He is a love I once knew"!!!

HE IS YOU!!!!

PASSION OF THE CHRIST!!!!

IT AIN'T GOT NOTHIN' ON YOU!!!

PASSION OF A MOTHER'S LOVE!!!!

The Universe at Work

My client at work has been misbehaving. She is attached to me. She knows on a level beyond the imagination that I will get done work.

She has been hitting out at me for the past two months. Not wanting me to leave. I do shift work. As I get ready for shift change she is having more behaviors than usual.

Change for her is extremely difficult. I feel bad. I know I must change jobs even though this will be devastating for her. Another beautiful soul who has suffered much. She has been a lesson in God's plan for all who touch her life.

It gets easier and easier for me to go to the astral planes for dream time. I see lines, circles and shapes. Many colors and awesome sights and wonderful lessons of life, love, faith and hope. It only takes mere minutes to go and I feel as if I am still awake.

My body still shakes for the angels I feel haven't let go of my body as I write about my whole experience. An amazing journey I must say. Will I sleep at all tonight? Probably not. Will I be o.k.? Yes, because God tells me rest one hour every day and be still and just love.

A long night and an early morning. My client knows I will be getting done work. I believe she hears the angels. Hers and mine.

My new career path I believe will be working with children. I will be learning as well as teaching. He shows me many choices. I can work at the mental facility. The hospital where I spent three tours of duty. I can work at the new center when the roof is raised and Felicia's wishes from the other side come to fruition. He even shows me a New Center not mentioned yet.

A task force put into place. Lost Soul Spirit Connections can start this center. God, Jesus, Mary and all that is Holy will support this center and with or without help it can BE a reality. He loves us that much and He believes in us that much. A missing children's center. Let's bring them home one at a time. With His love and Mary's grace we can do it together. They come to us now. Olivia waits, but fears her mother and father have forgotten her. They don't believe in Jesus. She wanders the planes. The five layers of the universe between Heaven and earth. She is lost and doesn't even know it. She is angry at her Mom and Dad. She is angry at God and she is angry for not knowing where she is or how to get home. I ask her to stand back. I ask her to be patient. I ask her to pray and ask Jesus and Mary for guidance and they will be there when she needs them most. She is another child taken too soon from this world. She has a connection with Ayla Faith. She was at Barbara Bush Center in Southern Maine with Ayla Faith when she was three months old. She shares with Cora her doctor was Scott. She shows Cora her pain. Cora feels sick. She has pain in her stomach. Olivia shows Cora she is angry and stubborn. Olivia shows Cora she has brown hair. It is in a long ponytail at the top of her head and to the side. Just like in my third eye.

Cora brings Olivia in immediately when I mention who I have seen in meditation. She and I have a gift to work together and God shares with us we can bring them home. We can put healing back into the lives and hearts of many.

Be patient and He will show us the way.

Another night of astral plane dreams. I know I am on another journey. I feel myself leave my body. I go floating through the atmosphere. It is not until I am back that I realize that I was in the Heavens again. Not just the astral planes.

I saw the face of Jesus Christ our Lord Savior, and the son of God.

A beautiful sight indeed. More breath taking than the portrait I saw so many years ago. An innocent child surrendering her heart to a man she knew nothing about.

Jesus I still love you!

He stands in the Heavens beautiful and majestic. He holds her hand. Little Miss Felicia. My breath catches in my throat and I cry. She is beautiful. No words are spoken. Just a knowing. She looks down as if seeing through to earth below. I see her blonde hair wispy and shiny. A flower entwined halo of daisies atop her head. Small pure white wings close to her tiny body. The same dress of vivid blue in my vision in the dark. I want her to look up. I want to see her smile. She is waiting patiently. Still for word from "Mommie". She asks "when, Meme, when"?

From the right St. Germain comes to me. He places my hands in his again, no words are spoken. I know he comforts me just by looking into my soul with his brilliant electric blue eyes. He is proud of how far I have come and he asks me if I could be patient just a little longer. This is a big mission and he has faith in me. He asks me to please have faith in Him (our father). I humbly smile and he knows I will. It is the whole reason I came back from the other side four years ago. A job for me has been revealed and I accept it and I will do my best. Patience is not one of my best suits.

I look down at Little Miss Felicia and it is an easy task. I think of my hero every time I dream of her or I see her beautiful smile and his teeth emerge one at a time. An earth angel saved for his own wonderful journey. A gift to us all.

Before I return I am shown a portrait or a picture. It is a picture I have seen before. I don't know who the artist is or where it is placed. It is famous. Two sensual hands. One reaching out to the other. Not quite touching. A beautiful portrait that when I see it I feel it is Jesus' hand is extended to one and all. Will they accept His invitation into His kingdom of glory or will they burn up into a ball of fire killing one another faster and faster as each day passes?

I am jerked out of sleep again. My heart pounding out of my chest and a headache like no other. It takes a while to come out of this revelation. This dream state is so huge. Amazing grace the song is given to me and I know Theresa's baby girl is here. Another angel taken too soon for a purpose greater than the human mind can grasp.

Humbled and brought to my knees again. Praying for strength and love strong enough to finish what needs to be done. Bring Felicia home one way or another. With or without help.

I am asked "please, be patient". "Your journey is an important part to the whole world". "Believing, keeping faith has been lost and I need you to be strong".

Mother Mary comes to me and I nod and wipe the tears away and pull myself together. I have life to live as I try to pull this miracle off one day at a time.

"Give me strength and protect me" I ask St. Michael. "Amen".

Clearing the air and I go for a walk.

Connecting with nature

Nature uses its magic as I struggle to move forward from yesterday. As I struggle with all of it. As I move forward from fear and as I move toward God's love and grace.

I am followed by a morning dove all the way on my walk today.

I try not to "think". Afraid if I stop the angels will flood my knowing and help me get closer to what I fear. The end! The goal! Bringing all of this to Trisha.

If I do then I will be proved. Will they prove me right or wrong? Will we find Felicia? Will they ignore me again? Will they call the people that have white coats, ready to strap me down? Medicate me? Make me sleep? Make me lose myself again to all of God's love and grace? I ask you Jesus???? Please, never shut out your beauty and all of my master teachers, my angels and all of the Little Miss Felicia's of the world.

I hear fireworks in the distance. Felicia shared with me from early communications that she wants a ticket tape parade on the 4th of July- she is coming home.

I hear bag pipes. They will be in the parade. She loves bag pipes.

As I arrive at my usual turning point where I met Charles Fillmore. My first teacher.

The message for this place is completed….

I must see this through to the end. For if I don't it won't reach Charles.

Prince Charles. Diana has been with me all along. She wants to help the children. Those that are suffering, dyeing and killing each other. Such a big message that is desperately needed to save our future children and the world.

I am reminded of my picture book. My rings. I am married to Christ. I am Mary. I am me, Bella. I stand before Him and I am three years old.

Just a child looking for hope, faith and His love and acceptance into the gates of Heaven.

In my meditation and dreams I am given many beautiful sights and many choices.

I choose to share all that He gives me. I choose to be a follower of Christ.

Princess Diana guides me with this learning center. She helps me as she stands with Little Miss Felicia and she has so many lost souls that stand with her.

Princess Diana shows me her ring. She has a beautiful sapphire ring. It is large in size and it is surrounded by many diamonds. I am not sure where she got this ring. She just shows me that it means the world to her. She asks me to share this in the book. To show that she is real and she is loved by God and all of His angels. She is still working her magic at the right side of God.

I see Mother Mary. I see Princess Diana. They are both guiding me with this huge project to help bring the children home. To help build this center for children that are in desperate need of a safe place to learn at their own pace.

A love for one child? No. A love for all of His children. A love for those who are still with us. A love for those who were lessons. A love for those who were blessings. A love for those who are still lost.

"I hear you can't make this stuff up". A great inspiration from a beautiful soul. Theresa Caputo….. A Truly amazing woman.

This message of faith, hope and love must reach all ports of call. Far and wide to get us out of all this hate and killing. Sacrifice is great!

He died for us.

He rose for us.

He is here every day!!!

Diana shows me she has Olivia's hand. Diana shows me she is with Felicia.

Another day! Another break!

Felicia chimes in, "Meme goes for a walk".

As I try to regroup and take back my life the sun is shining and it's going to be 80 degrees today. I have the day off and I am going to take care of me.

I stop and peek at my pine tree. The largest tree on my property. I envision Chelsey at the top. My eagle. My closest and dearest animal to God. The eagle.

The sun warms my entire body as I stand on my deck. I close my eyes and I see the angels surround me. Pinpoint dots. I see them as my eyes are closed. My sign that my angels are with me.

I open my eyes and I see her. My Chelsey, my eagle, my God. She spreads her wings and she takes off.

Chelsey reminds me of the day of her funeral. Carol and I sit on her Grandmothers porch. On the swing. We sit, we cry and we reconnect after an overdue absence from one another. Carol and I try to find solace in one another's company. We talk and tears flow freely.

The wind chimes start to sing. The wind is still. Not a breeze in the air. A chill runs up my spine and the hair on my neck is alive.

Carol and I both grab one another's hands and the tears come again and we smile. Chelsey is with us and we both knew it instantly.

She was a loss for me that ripped so many hearts apart. She helped me write my first book Miracles among Chaos. Ten years later she still helps me write in journaling and all of my books. Thank you sweetie. I love you. <3

After my morning "hello" to Chelsey, I go for my walk.

I hit the first driveway. My neighbor, "Casey at bat". He lost his dad this winter.

A blue jay is in his driveway. My little Miss Felicia. Blue is the color for communication and she is my little blue jay.

Little Miss Felicia has been trying for nearly eight months to come home to her mother. It's all in God's hands now honey. Be patient and if it's meant to be it will happen.

As Little Miss Felicia flies away, she turns into a morning dove. Yes, right before my eyes the blue jay turns into a morning dove. Believe it or leave it! All of it!!

The morning dove is my connection to two special men in my life. The two Charlies'. One a father figure I loved completely like no other. The other a brother figure and best friend. Taken too soon from this world. Another tragedy. Another loss I struggle to understand.

I smile and just enjoy the gifts that God has given me and I walk on. Clearing my head and my heart of Felicia's case. Letting go is never easy.

On my way home I run into a porcupine. I video tape part of my walk and he climbs the apple tree where I stand and close my eyes. The place where I have gone back in time.

The porcupine represents my writing. The quills are to represent my pen and it is sharp and steep. A vision in developing my gifts the weekend before. Meditation with Angel connections a group I reach out to as I try to understand this journey just a little more.

I am surrounded by dragon flies and they fill the air as I get closer to the end of my walk. The dragon flies represent my father. All the fathers gone before mine. To the beginning of time. The first time I realized my father was with me after his death. I stood in my back yard and the air was filled with black and silver dragon flies.

As I walk the long dirt road a single dragon fly lands on my chest. The long dirt road is where I find sanctuary in nature. I find peace of mind and reconnect to my heart and to God. Praise be to His name.

A Mother's Love

As I continue with my own inner struggles. Letting go of my own desires. My own wants and needs. They do not serve God's best interests. I am shown so many choices and I fear the most, letting Him down.

Mary, Mother Mary. Jesus' mother. She sacrificed so much for the love of her Son. No sacrifice is too great for the love of a child. I get this over and over and over in my life time.

I struggled through my own marriage with feeling like I needed to protect my own children. I was even ridiculed for trying to protect my own children too much. Is it a defect caused by my own childhood traumas and drama's or was I just being the best mother I could be?

Through God's mercy and grace I have my eyes open to so much love. So many gifts of His own sacrifice for God's children.

Mother Mary sacrifice's her own son. Ridiculed by many for her immaculate conception. She was chosen for a great purpose. A gift of life and a gift of love. Straight from God.

No different in my eyes than any one of us. We are all God's children and we all have a special purpose in this life. To love to the best of our ability.

Mother Mary comes to me daily now. She has always been with me as have all of my Angels, teachers and my Master. Our Lord, Father and God. Jesus Christ our Savior and Lord.

He lives as does Mother Mary and all of our angels. Within each of us.

Ridicule me. Doubt me. Fear the words I write. Please never stop believing in His LOVE. Please never stop hoping. Please never stop surrendering your fear. For fear is what freezes each one of us in our own tracks and paralyzes us in our own self-hate, self-doubt and this is where we can tend to lose His love and His light. We become lost and so many of us struggle to find a way back.

Being a mother is the reason I cannot. Will not give up this gift of communication with my angels. I will not give up on Little Miss Felicia. I will never give up until God thanks me for doing my best.

A mother's love to the end. Mary's. My own. I believe in my heart that even Felicia's mom someday will understand the how, why and why not's of why I could not give up on her beautiful baby girl.

Mother Mary shows me she was with me in the hospital. She heard my cries. "Mummah, Mummah, Mummah." "Help me, help me, help me."

Over and over again for nearly 6 hours. I cried these three words. I couldn't speak anything else. The pain was so great. I was dying. Mother Mary knew this and so did I.

I only remember the pain. Unbearable pain.

I wasn't scared. I was just in so much pain.

I remember the doctors coming in and going out. They would check on me. Go out. I would move very little. Hang off the edge of the rails of the bed and holler...... Mummah, Mummah, Mummah. Help me!!!

She tells me. "You have paid a high price for His love for so long". "He will prove you". "He will help you". "Your angels will help you".

"Little Miss Felicia" will come home". Mother Mary's words are encouraging and I love her for that.

I am taxed and they know it. I am tired and my emotions are spent.

Today I made the decision it is time. Cora and I will go to search for Felicia. We will bring her home.

Spiritual Law of Attraction

As I figure out all of God's gifts. His love shines through with this project. Ayla Faith's Learning Center. He helps me to find peace within myself. Cora and I will bring Little Miss Felicia home.

A great teacher who is with me always shows up all day today. Melchizedek. He is stern looking and his eyes pierce through to my soul. He shows me the love I have for Jesus and Mary are great and the price for all of my pain and suffering will be paid in full.

Lightening has been striking around the world for far too long. Children have been suffering and it is time to bring some hope and faith back to God's children. Those who have a glimpse and a glimmer of hope still in their eyes will have it shinning bright again.

Hearts will heal.

The spiritual Law of Attraction has been set in motion and it comes from the hope, faith and love of my own dreams and my own spiritual journey finding God.

Holistic healing is such a big peace of my connecting with Jesus and Mary and all of my high angels. My Master's. My teacher's and my earth angel connections. Those who were so innocent and some not so innocent. All were lessons within a blessing.

As I learn from the best of the best I bring all of the gifts that I have seen go into the atmosphere. They will come back to me.

It may not happen in my time frame. They tell me time does not matter. Not when God is involved. It is an ongoing cycle. Life.

Reincarnation is true and real.

Jesus' second incarnate is my master of all teacher's. St. Germain. He tells me to work my magic and bring this child home.

They will all be with me. My master teacher's. My angels. Jesus and Mary.

Cora's teachers and angels will be with her.

Felicia's angels. Her own band of special angels. Her family members who have crossed over from this lifetime and those of high ranking stand by her side always and forever. Loving and protecting her. Another lesson. Another blessing. His little lamb. Just a gift for us for a short time. Taken to show proof of His love.

Meme will be there soon sweetie. To bring you home to Mommie and Puppa!!!!!

Hold on tight. Hold His hand and pray for His light to shine bright through all of our love. For He is God and He is GOOD.....

Back To The Mount

OLD COMRADES

I WALKED AMONG MY COMRADES BRAVE UPON THAT BLOODY HILL AND SAW NO MOVEMENT. None at all, for it was deathly still. There were no cries from trembling lips. No soldier's blasphemy. I call their names out. Every one. But no one answered me. I know each rock. Each clump of trees that marks this hallowed ground for in my mind I see them fall and hear that battle sound but now the silence takes my breath for all that I can see are rows on rows of crosses where old comrades used to be.

Thomas Lynn-Korean war veteran

June 23, 2016

Truly amazing. Revelations every day. Miracles to happen. Miracles have happened. He is risen. He is present within each and every one of us.

Felicia and I go to Mt. Hope cemetery again. This is our third visit.

Our first visit was for her ascension to be with Jesus. She was stuck. She is free now. She is by Jesus' side. An angel of pure beauty.

Felicia has me pull over to the memorial. We get out and go over to the entrance where the flags fly high and they are numerous. Colorful flags and Felicia jumps for joy. She loves her country like no other child I have seen.

She loves the veterans. Men and women who sacrificed so much for their families and their country.

I become uneasy quickly. I am surrounded by spirit. I feel it so strong and I for the first time realize this gift is a blessing and I absolutely love it.

The body sensations are overwhelming.

I walk slowly over the stones leading to the shiny black wall. The list of names on this beautiful memorial, there are so many. I could never begin to count them all.

There are names and messages that are in stone beneath my feet. It is as if I feel their names through my shoes and they all want to connect with someone. Loved ones that miss them and loved ones that are wondering how they are and if they are by God's side.

As I strain to walk on. Their presence within me becomes overwhelming. My ears are filled with them. They all try to get messages of names and things they want said.

My neck seems heavy and it seems to meld into one with my shoulders. Some of these spirits are so desperate to get messages to loved ones. Lost souls here on earth. Sad and lonely missing them. Left alone to spend their last days by themselves. Sad. Very sad. I push the tears back and Felicia and I hold hands and walk on.

Through all this emotion I hear them. I hear the angels and I hear the organ begin to play. It is huge and so beautiful. I look around to see if I can see a loud speaker and there is none. I have been to this cemetery many times and never have I heard the soft flowing music of the organ before.

The tune is familiar but I cannot place it. I have heard it in the church. St. John's church.

As Felicia and I walk slowly toward the wall. I see men and women from all walks of life. I see Marines, I see airmen, and I see foot soldiers and some I don't even recognize what era or time they are from.

There are uniforms of blue, green, white and tan. They stand at attention and they salute us. Why I do not know. We are nothing. I am nothing. Just a girl who is on a journey I struggle to hold onto reality as He shows me His love.

Some soldiers, men and women. Some black, some white and some even Korean descent. So many nationalities. I have never been one to judge what color the skin is and He whispers to me now, "It never mattered". "Not then." "Not now". "Just love one another".

Some are lost. Some of these poor souls are wearing tattered uniforms. They are bloody and their clothes have holes. I feel a bullet. It strikes my right shoulder blade and I feel more pain in my heart than in my left shoulder. This is where Jesus feels pain each time a child, young or old is taken from the world. Brought back to Him for another journey. Another lifetime. To help in His work. To help share blessings and lessons among all that He has created.

These are pains I feel throughout my body. Times that are becoming more evident as I get closer and more confident in this journey.

I see, feel, hear, smell and taste it all. All of my senses are awake to the spirit world. God's beauty. In disguise for so many. I am awake and I am good.

He shows me more and more. My gifts. I can travel back in time.

I can travel forward in time.

I can be present in the moment.

I am given things. The future. It is very dim right now.

Jesus is scared and that is why He is present. So strong and desperately trying to wake us all up.

Yesterday Jean Dixon visited me. I struggle in writing this. Who am I? No one. Just a girl.

He whispers "Who loves very much".

Jean Dixon. A counsel too many back in her day.

Presidents and ministers alike sought her council.

Jean is proud of me. My faith and love. She tells me I am so much like her. I am a see'er. God's special earth angel.

Again I am humbled. Believe it or leave it.

Jean Dixon shares with me the next president.

A name. Another one going down in the books. History in the making.

Why because she too was a P.O.W.

A child lost. One with great strength and love for God. A faith unending in human kind.

Hillary Clinton will be the next PRESIDENT of the UNITED STATES OF AMERICA!!

Why…..Because HE said so!

I am showed so much in just one visit. So many souls. Lost souls and souls just wanting to connect with loved ones.

He knows it is so much for one person to take in but He knows how strong my faith is and how much I want to bring Felicia home to her mother.

I smile and tell Him please take me to her resting place.

Felicia and I walk and Princess Diana joins us and I hear the cardinal join us and we walk slowly to the mount. To the top it is a haul. As we go around the pond and see all the lily pads Felicia reminds me of our first visits. She shows me lily's around the house. The beacon for Cora and me to find her when we go to the store where she was still alive.

There are several tiny black birds sitting on the lily pads. I have to wonder. How do these birds sit on top of these lily pads? I would think they are too heavy and the lily pads would sink.

Some things I am shown are not truly so. Just His magic. The organ music was from Heaven. It was not real. A gift from God and His angels.

Felicia and I climb the hill and the hill turns into stone. Granite stone steps and they go up as far as the eye can see.

My legs are heavy and the path on each side of the steps leading to the mount are lined with souls. Spirits that have passed. Men and women some in uniform. Some in dresses and suits. So many children. They stand alone, they stand together. Families buried so long ago. Years gone by and missed and loved. Some forgotten.

Felicia and I reach the top and I see the burning bush. The same one I saw just before I released her to Jesus last fall. Back in November of 2015.

The berries are not present. It is too early. Another sign she has shown me for so long. The red berries I associated with holly and Christmas. Jesus' birthday. She still wants Jesus in her life and the life of all children. She shares with me let those children who want Jesus to pray with them, learn with them to let Him be in their life.

As she finishes with this message of her wishes from the other side on this special project I hear a man screaming in the background. In the distance.

She pulls on my arm. She tells me it's him. I don't believe she met him. It is her grandfather. She never met him. Her father's father. Another lost soul. Mean as a rabid dog. She shares with me.

Jesus shows me a lamb. In his arms. He carries a lamb in His arms.

As Felicia and I stop. My heart flips in my chest and I know. The reason for this.

John, the grandfather. Is this from one, two or three generations back? I am not truly sure. I feel it is one. It could be further back....

I hear him cough. He has a hard time breathing. He shows me he has a fluid issue. CHF maybe. He is drowning in his own misery. Sadness no one else knows about.

He is not with Jesus. He is lost in between worlds. He is in the astral planes. Stuck like Felicia was but on a different plane. Darker and colder than where she was. Sad and alone. Paying for his sins. Still today.

She pulls me to her resting place. She is eager to sit with me and place her special things on her favorite spot on Mt. Hope cemetery's beautiful plots.

Early that morning before shopping for groceries Felicia goes to the dollar tree with me. I knew before we walked through the door what she wanted. She wanted a wreath of red white and blue. I knew I would find it. I knew where I would find it.

She is like most all other little girls. When we go into the store she wanted more. She makes me laugh and we buy a heart shaped wreath of red, white and silver. We also buy a heart shaped flag on a stick with streamers. She pulls me to the flowers and she tells asks me "please". For the lady in red.

Felicia wants to buy lilies for Princess Diana. Her mother figure in heaven a beautiful soul that loved children and worked so hard to meet the needs of so many while she was with us.

How can you refuse such an angel? I pick up light pink day lilies. That is what I see when I see Princess Diana. Felicia says "no". She pulls me to the white tiger lilies. We pick them up and take them to the register.

An amazing child. An amazing woman. An amazing pair.

Back on the mount. Mt. Hope cemetery Felicia and I write a little in her message book to mommie.

A picture of a tiger stripped kitten sleeping. She helped me pick this special book out for her mother. She has messages in it for only Mommie. A secret. A love that will never end for her mother.

Felicia and I say a prayer. We rest and we lay beside her father's stone. A stone she pretends is for when he joins her someday.

Princess Diana stands by the big pine tree. She overlooks the cemetery and waits for Felicia. Lady Di' knows she is excited to connect again with her mother. I know in my heart there is no turning back now. Cora and I will go to bring her home.

As I lay in the grass next to the stones I close my eyes and I breathe in and I smell the cedar trees and the pine trees. What a glorious day. I wish I could do this every day. Spend the day with angels and listen to God's words and see all of His beauty.

As I lay their next to such a pure angel I feel like my heart is laying on my chest. Not within my body. I feel it beat deep and the blood flows. I feel so connected with Jesus that it's as if I feel His blood flowing through my own veins.

As I lose myself and tears flow from all the love I feel in my heart. A dragon fly lands on my chest. I feel it and I jump. I open my eyes and it is black. His body is black and parts of his wings are pure white. My Dad. The dragon fly. Dad is with us.

I smile and he flies away.

I lay back and I look up at the clouds. There are white fluffy clouds and I rest my eyes. I wasn't long closing my eyes and I am startled again. A fluttering on my third eye. A beautiful large butterfly. A light cocoa brown butterfly lands on my forehead.

She flits up, straight up. I know immediately it is my hero's grandmother. I woman I never met. She has been with me for a while. How long I don't know. Sam's mother. Eleanor. A lost soul while here, yes. Taken too soon, yes. "A good mother and a wonderful woman". I am given by God and Mary.

Lessons learned are hard. Blessings are in abundance. The lessons are out weighing the blessings and He wants to give back something. He wants to give back a child taken from this world to her mother and he will let us bring her home.

To bring hope, faith and love back. Not all will be returned. Not all lessons can be erased. He will shine His light on a few and He hopes for a miracle. Will this child be able to bring hope back? She is hope for those who have searched for her. She is hope for those who felt all the pain surrounded by her suffering. Will this make a difference or will this miracle be over looked like those that He allows us to experience every day.

He shows me the rainbow. A promise from many years ago. Never to flood the world again.

He shows me the double rainbow. He shares this is the sign for a wish. A wish made by so many. A gift is given back in the double rainbow. Not very often. Sometimes the pain is too great and He does give us huge miracles like this one.

Little Miss Felicia will come home!!!!

Praise His name and I make plans to bring her home and I pray my faith and love is true enough to make this miracle of His come true......

As Felicia and I pick up and come down from the mount. She asks me to bring a few things back to our God box. She shows me cedar trees and I pick a large piece for our God box. As we come down the granite stone steps a squirrel runs in front of us and Felicia says "squirrel"..... I laugh and she giggles. My heart swells and I can only imagine how much her mother must miss her.

When we get to the grass Felicia shows me two feathers....

They are light brown and fluffy. They remind me of chicken feathers. They remind me of Cora and me. Young at heart and full of love.

"Am I chicken"? "Will I for fill this prophecy" He asks.

"Yes I will". "If you will"?

I say yes to His questions as I become more confident.

A nagging fear still peaks its head up and I am angry at myself....

He forgives me for my fear. He knows I always wait for the worst. It is a cross that I have carried for so long.

Felicia see's Princess Diana standing next to a black gated plot. She stands next to a rusted old bench. The lady in red urges her to come. It is time for Felicia to go home.

She looks up and she blows me a kiss. I reach out and I grab the air. I catch her kiss and I eat it....

She giggles and she is gone.

I try to center myself as I stand there and my heart hurts. I can only imagine what her mother must be going through. Felicia comes to me more often now than she has in the first of our communication. It's like I don't want her to go the closer we get to the end.

Tears come and I know once she connects with her mom she won't need me anymore. She will be gone and I wonder what will be true and what will not be.

I walk down the incline and a fire catches my eye. My tears are still on my lashes and I see into the fire. Mt. Hope cemeteries garage door is open and I see someone stirring the fire.

Someone is in the oven.

"REALLY"!!!!

I say it out loud and I feel sick to my stomach. After all I have done and after all of my pain He shows me someone in the flipping oven!!!!

I ask "how much more". I don't need to see any more…..

I want to bring her home. He knows I am ready. He knows Cora is ready.

A fire in the pot. A fire under my ass. A fire in my heart and a fire in my soul.

He shows it all to me. He knows I can handle whatever He puts in front of me. My faith and my love IS that great.

Not just another trip to the cemetery….

A revelation beyond anything like it!

Praise be to GOD………………………………

Taking it outside

A marriage is a bond like no other. Another reminder of my love for Jesus and we fight.

I hear Him whisper "You are working too hard again". "Go out side". "Refresh yourself".

I sit for hours typing today's messages of love and feel all of these emotions over take my entire being.

Jesus is frustrated with me again. For working too hard and yet I sit at the computer again to write it all down before I forget the love I feel for Him is real and I laugh at him and I laugh at myself. I am as stubborn as Little Miss Felicia and I don't give in easily.

I want to bring her home yesterday....

That didn't happen....

I want to bring her home tomorrow....

That won't happen....

"Patience child".....

I am tired and frustrated and He knows it. I am taxed to the max and He truly loves me for all of it.

I picture in my mind's eye finding her. I pick up wood. Little pieces and I see them....

They are her bones. There are no maggots. There is no decayed flesh. There are no opened eyes....Empty eye sockets like I have seen so many times in my lifetime.

I thank God for that. At least I won't have nightmares about finding her like that.

I am strong and I have seen a lot of stuff and I have been preparing with all of my visions of death and destruction over my life times for this moment.

I picture finding her. I work with Melchizedek and the spiritual law of attraction. Think it, feel it and believe it. Believe in Him. Have faith in Him and He will allow miracles to happen.

Melchizedek asks me "please find the blessings in your situation".

It becomes easier the closer I become one with God.

Apollo comes on my "time out"… My walk into nature if you will.

He comes to me in my dreamtime. He is handsome and strong and I love all of God's gifts. They are blessing's each one of His high master teacher's and His angels on high.

Apollo tells me "focus on your strength's"…

My love and my heart beat wildly for His love and acceptance. So I have opened it….

A can of worms? No a passion deeper than that of THE PASSION OF THE CHRIST!!

Serapis Bey joins us and he tells me "Go Now"…..

Not right now. But soon. Plan and listen. Watch and learn.

Jesus and my angels, high and low will let me know when it is time.

"Soon" is what I am given….

Cora and I are ready.

I see him coming down the road. He is great in size and he is adorned with jewels and a crown of beauty. Ganesh is the Hindu elephant-headed "over comer of obstacles" who clears paths for miracles to happen. He has been with me since October and probably before that. He shares with me wisdom in my writing and loves all of my passion for Christ.

I thank them all for such wisdom and support. As I try to pull myself together they all nod and leave me to be alone.

I walk out back and I look for something I am not sure what. I keep seeing Felicia everywhere I go. I keep seeing the same scenes over and over and it is not pretty.

I end up in the corner by the fence. I see a rock. I see a tree. I see her but I can't get to her.

In the corner by the post He comes. He asks "why do you love so much?"

I ask Him "why do you test me so much?"

I look into His eyes and I want kiss Him…..

"I just want to find her".

"I just want to bring her home to her mother".

"I want healing to happen for so many".

He tells me that is exactly what He wants. He is glad we are on the same page.

I back Him into the corner and I turn on Him. I step into His space and I become one with Him.

He allows it and I show Him I am the boss and He shows me it's o.k. for me to think I am the boss!!!!

I laugh. I know it is Him and I as one and we play as we fight and both of us will win no matter what happens.

He knows I am saved and I know for the first time I am loved unconditionally for all of my love.

A marriage made in heaven and we are both satisfied with the outcome of his plan no matter what happens tomorrow.

PROCLIVITY- a word that is thrown my way. I don't know whether it is even a real word. It takes a few days but it keeps coming to me and I finally write it down and I finally search the internet for its meaning:

Proclivity- 1- An inclination or predisposition toward something; especially: a strong inherent inclination toward something objectionable. 2-A strong natural proneness usually to something objectionable or evil. 3-a natural inclination.

Nearing the end or starting at the beginning?

For the past eight months I never know which it is. I can travel to the past with past life regression. In the same moments…. I can travel to the future.

I can see much and it is wonderful. I sometimes don't know whether my life is just starting or ending. I am not an easy soul to understand and Jesus agrees.

I spend the day with my niece Raina. Another light worker who struggles with her gifts. She is fifteen years old and she is brilliant and beautiful. Spirit has come to her since she was nine. Her first close loss. The same loss for me. In a different context though. A true friend and a soulmate.

As Raina and I start our day together Felicia and Theresa come to spend the day with us. They are together a lot. Throughout the communications of eight months. Both beautiful angels and they both are blessings in their lessons. Hard to understand God's plan but He knows that which we don't. The plan He set before us before time began.

We go to the mount again. Felicia wishes for Raina to witness where she was released and she wants the world to see her special place that Meme released her to be with Jesus. She twirls and whirls and she giggles. She has a plan. Her and God. A secret. She tells me Raina doesn't know it but God has a special plan for her. I know what it is but I will not share all of His love with you. Some things are better left for secrets….. Raina must learn, trust and love Jesus for His plan to be optimal benefit for her.

I share with Raina most of the beautiful things that transpired during Felicia's and my first visits to the mount. Mt. Hope cemetery…..

We climb the steep stone steps and we go the long way and Felicia shows me a new sign. One I have seen before but not on this trail. She shows me a cable and a flag and posts. It is a trail closed off. Is this a true sign that the road that leads to her is closed off or is it just what it is?

Somethings I struggle with as I learn all of my signs and symbols and struggle to trust the Lord. He is frustrated and so am I. He with me? Maybe. He with the world? Definitely.....

I struggle more with myself than He does with me. He knows my faith and He knows my love is an unending story. Communication with the spirit world has happened since the beginning of time. The Bible has revealed it. Jesus did it way back when and it is time to listen and hear the wonders from the other side. Loved ones who have passed and loved ones who are lost on both sides of heavens doors.

Jesus loves me this I know....

I start today's love letters in the sand at the end of my day. So much information and I am exhausted.

I retreat into nature and I try to center myself and refresh. We end our walk with my favorite church hymn "Jesus loves me this I know for the Bible tells me so".

There were so many children tonight. They are excited for Felicia as they all wait their turn. In hopes that they will get a turn. To give messages to their loved ones or to maybe even get a chance to come home.

Felicia is disappointed because I am asked to wait a little longer. I am asked to take one last chance and maybe open the eyes of a close friend. A gentleman who has lost a little angel of his own.

Amy.....

She has been with me for a while now. I am not sure if her father even knows her name. She was taken before she had time to fully grow. A miscarriage and it still doesn't hurt any less than if you lost them at age two, three or fifty-two.

I am given that she was named after her death. I can only ask and I struggle with this. Such an emotional time for two very special people. They are well aware of the spirit world and I am asked to go one last time to let the proper authorities know that Courtney and I will be going to look for Felicia.

Carl is a cop. He may be able to help. Maybe not. I am asked to try. So I will. Jesus knows I will do anything He asks so again, disappointment on my part and sadness in Felicia's eyes that hurts beyond belief.

Another sleepless night? Maybe....

Felicia has experienced a couple of disappointments over the past two days and I tell her I am sorry. She wanted to get an ice cream yesterday with me and I ended up going home. I was too tired. Again today, no ice cream with Raina and I. She smiles and she says it's o.k. but I see the disappointment.

On our walk with all of her friends, angels taken too soon she has me pick daisies and she wants a ring, a halo made. I pick a big bunch and she stands among the flowers and holds Amy's hand.

The other angels, just babies some of them play in the tall grass. Boys and girls alike. What a beautiful sight. Never will I forget such a blessing as this in my life. God is good and he has shown me such a magnificent sight today.

I go back to the river today. I am drawn after a wonderful morning with Raina.

I am reading the bible again as I try to refresh and just take a few minutes to reflect and look at the bible that I received from Charles. My wonderful friend who was with me when I went to heaven the first time. The day I decided to come back for this special project.

I sit and read the bible and I find so many passages outlined and highlighted and there are messages in the book and I have no idea who wrote some of them. I can only assume it was one of the angels. Too many messages to even try to go into. They are prophetic and amazing. They hit home on so many levels with all that is going on now and back during the time the good book was written. Such hate and destruction is rampant today.

Racial issues are still over running this country and the world. Famine and homelessness. Such pain is evident everywhere. Children are dyeing and killing other children.

When will we wake up and let God lead us once again?

Finding her way

I finish looking at the bible and I am guided to the left. I stretch first and breathe in the air. I smell the trees and I smell the water. I hear the birds and I see the blue skies. The sun is getting ready to go down over the high rocks across the street and I go down the path toward the water.

As I descend down over the hill I see the water below. I stop short and fear hits me. I see it. This path I feel is familiar and at the bottom I am shown a snake. I don't believe we have this type of snake in Maine. It is fairly large and it is reared up and stands up a little. It almost reminds me of a cobra, but it was smaller.

I know what I am being shown. I stop and my skin crawls. I see her father's face and I can't walk any further.

I raise my hands to my head and I pull at my hair. I know in my heart I am not coming to the river to have a leisurely walk. I am going to see things I know I don't want to see.

I motion after a few minutes. I ask my angels to show me more. My master teachers and my earth angels alike. I ask for nature to work its magic and let me see where she is.

I stand and I wait. I am guided to turn left. I stand and I am shown. The rock wall….

I am shown the base of a tree….

I am shown a hill…..

These I have seen more times than I can count. I have brought my camera and I take a picture. I see the orb…. It is Felicia on my camera. Amazing and beautiful. God's magic and confirmation enough for me. This is what it looks like where she is.

I am guided down the hill after I pull myself together and I feel the sting on my left leg. I am struck by the snake…. A bite. Not in reality, but to show that I should not go down near the water.

I swat at my leg because it hurt.

To my left I see it. The blanket. It lays on the rocks. It is not blue, it is a tan color. In spirit world communication sometimes numbers and colors are not true to their meaning. They just lead you closer to your messages. I take a picture. Evidence enough for me to help me on my journey to finding Felicia and bringing her home.

I go closer to the water. I see where I am. It is the "river Jordan". Not literally… Metaphorically speaking. The child that was sacrificed for a greater good. To hopefully save another child's life. In the greater plan, His plan…..

I stand next to the river and I see rocks stacked. One on top of the other. Not in just one place but in 3 separate places. For me this leads me to believe she is near the rock wall, under the rock wall or buried.

I look to the left and I see almost chunk like blocks of cement or stone. There are two of these. I take a picture with the one closest to the water. I am lead to set my bible next to the one with the rock inside the tunnel. For some reason Princess Diana comes to mind. Maybe a lesson maybe not. Maybe that will be revealed later.

I take a picture of the tunnel further away and I get that she keeps saying "so close yet so far"….. She means the cops have looked high and low and yet they still have not brought justice to her terrible tragedy.

I hear her in the distance…..

She cries and she says "hurry Meme"………

"It is tight and it is dark"……

"It is wet and damp and I am scared here"…..

"I want to go home to be with mommie"…………

I stand by the river and I cry.

I don't know how long it takes me to come back to reality. Messages from the other side and I want to take my car and I want to go to where Felicia asks me to start the search. She asks Cora and me to start at the store where she stopped last for a candy bar.

The guy with the letter "S"?……

Is this even anyone? It was so early in my teachings and learning of my signs and symbols for mediumship that I wonder at this point.

I still get best bud/cousin. He looks similar but taller than Dad.

I get a name…. Jason? Is this the best bud?

I still get Gram had a hand in it. How does a mother not know her own child?????

The rest will come together….

Someone will turn on the other……

It doesn't matter anyway…..

"Just bring her home". Charles chimes in, "The man wants her home".

I go to the spot where the tree is. I stop as I am guided to. My phone is in my pocket I pull it out and I fear I won't be able to get the video I want.

The documentary I am asked to record for her mother…

For the cops….

For someone to please open the damn door and help us bring her home.

I get just enough as usual to know that I am good for this piece of it. I gather my senses and I take it all in and I wait for any more information that my teachers/masters may have….

Nothing.

I ask the angels if there is any more? Nothing.

I listen and I walk back up the hill and I am so glad to leave. I turn on the radio and I try to detox and refresh and I cry and I play with my angels and I play with Jesus and Mary.

I am good and I am grounded and He tells me He loves me for loving her so much.

I will never give up on her.

I will never give up on her center. Ayla Faith's Learning Center. I will never give up on Jesus Christ our Lord God and Savior……

Miracles on Broadway

Fund raising day for the center. Her center. Her last wish. Meme's big project. A production in the making.

Raina and I get up early and we head out after my nature walk. I am looking forward to His grace, mercy and love today and He proves me right yet again……

The plan for the day was to do a bottle drive from 10 a.m. to 4 p.m. No such luck.

Our first stop was amazing. God's connections and love put to work right off the bat. He reminds me to trust up and I do. He says thank you for all of my hard work.

After a wonderful short visit with Larry, an earth angel and a veteran Raina and I drive off with a full load of bottles. From ceiling to floor front to back. What a score indeed.

After talking to Larry and telling him some of the plans for the center and him reading a poem that Felicia and I wrote back in February. He is moved and he asks me one question….

How long did it take for you to write this poem? A day? Three days? I said "no".

"It didn't even take ten minutes". I explained to him that I use what I call automatic writing. A type of connection with the inner self. My higher consciousness. My connection to my angels and to God.

The more I exercise my writing the better it becomes. The more I interact with my angels, teacher and masters the more I open the doors to the spirit world. The more I connect with nature the better messages I get and the better see' er I will become. Connecting to God and all of his wonders. What a great gift indeed.

Just before leaving I give Larry a wrist bracelet. A thank you from Lost Soul Spirit Connections to a great contributor to the world. A man with a heart of gold.

Larry and his wife donated $100 to Ayla Faith's Learning Center. A great start for a great cause. Children with learning disabilities and the demand becomes greater every day.

I am guided after an hour and a half into the bottle drive "It is complete". "Stop pushing yourself and go home"…..

I heed His words and I stop.

Closing In

June 25, 2016

Walking it off and still searching for His truth. Connecting again with my own heart and His.

I walk this lonely road yet again. It will not be the last walk and it will not be the last of the messages of beauty, hope, faith and LOVE!!

I am totally surrounded by children. Spirits and angels. High and low in ranking. God's children. From days gone by. From days to still come.

Reincarnation is given to me yet again. I have lived other lifetimes and I believe with all of my heart I will come again. I will rise out of these ashes and tears of sadness for this lost child. I will let God take her and I will have faith and I will Love Him until the ends of time.

I soak in the early evening sunshine. It is slowly setting beyond the tall grass and the far away trees. I hear the morning dove still and it is almost time for bed. My two Charles are checking in with me to make sure I stay on His path. Not to falter and never to fail.

I can do no wrong from this point on. My love for Him is too great and His love for me is never ending.

I raise my arms up and I feel St. Germain. He stands beside me and they slowly come closer. The high saints, the master teachers. One by one they know I love like no other. I trust and I have found my true meaning for life.

Just LOVE! Just BE! BE-LOVED!!

I walk home and I see her by the farmhouse. She sticks her nose out from the tree branches.

Felicia is playing in the trees. She is a small elephant. She hangs upside down from the tree. She plays alone and she waits for Meme to find her. I stop and look up at her. I feel the breeze become stronger and I breathe it in.

I feel her love and I see it. She tells me. "Meme, remember me". "Even if no one else does, I know you will always remember me".

I look up and tears flow down my face. She breaks my heart yet again. She has FAITH unending in Jesus and she has faith in me.

She loves her mother so much and I know that kind of love. Mother Mary has been so good and so beautiful. To all of His children. She is with them all watching and loving them until they can be with their earth mother's. Mother Mary will be with Little Miss Felicia until you can find it in your heart to love and feel His light and join Him on the other side.

I blow her a kiss and she catches it. A game we play when it is time to go. I love this child and what a complete doll she is. Those electric blue eyes haunt my sleep and I pray to never lose her love. Time is closing in for all of us and that is what this whole book is about.

He is coming and He is trying prepare us. Are you ready?

Rocks of Gibraltar

June 26, 2016

I wake up and I am ready for a test drive. I pack my bags and no one knows my true plans for the day except for my Lord, God and Savior. Jesus Christ. The love of my life. My SAVING GRACE!!!

I struggle with whether I should tell someone where I am going. He says "no". "You're good".

I listen like a good girl….

He says "thank you". Time and time again.

He says "You love too much".

He says "I love you so much".

He says "That's all I ever ask of anyone".

I go with God's grace and I am prepared for only what He wants.

I know what I want and I know what Felicia wants. I need to trust up and I do. He is amazed by my faith in Him.

I get to her hometown and I let the angels guide me everywhere I go. Trusting in Jesus is such an amazing feeling. I listen to Him with an open heart and He leads me to the parking lot.

I take only what He tells me to bring. Nothing.

Second thought….

I bring water…

I bring her diaper bag….

I bring my phone….

I'm ready to bring her home. I feel her and she is so excited. I hear her and I can't wait to find her.

I follow the railroad tracks and I am guided to go off the tracks. I see the water tower….

It is a smoke stack I see. An old building on the other side of the river. There is a foot bridge and I stop before I go down to it. I listen and I feel the pull. He wants me to go across the river. I listen and one foot in front of the other and I read all the signs. I listen to all of my angels.

I am lead by the heart to where she is. I see her. Not Felicia. I see Princess Diana. I hear her singing softly. "Then sings my soul, my Savior God to thee"...... What a beautiful sight and what a beautiful day.

In anticipation of mentally preparing myself for what is sure to be a miracle I push my emotions to the side and I push my fears deep down like I have done for years.

I am guided to go up the steep hill. I am then guided to go back down the other side. Just like at Mt. Hope cemetery.

I ask Felicia "where are you sweetie?" "Meme needs you to help me find you".

I am drawn back down to the tarred road. Then I see it. The entrance into the woods. I take a deep breath and one step in front of the other.

I push my way through. I go left and I go up. I listen to the crow at the top of the hill. I find a large stick to use to help me keep my footing and I go up the steep hill.

I stop and I catch my breath. I see the tree. As I get closer I feel it. Confirmation that I am right. I get confirmation that He does love me.

I stand in front of the tree that she showed me yesterday. It is much larger than the tree she showed me yesterday. At the base of the tree there is a large entrance into the tree. It is almost large enough for a small child to stand in. There is a tire. Black and rubber sitting in front of the tree. There is much decay on this tree it is dead. All the way up to the top.

I am told "No, Bella". "Not quite". I take a deep breath in and I become a little frustrated.

I feel the pull to the right. My body goes first and then my eyes. I see three large trees uprooted and tipped over. I have seen these in dreams, meditation and in my walks.

I walk closer to the edge and my heart drops to bottom of the tall drop off. I see the water fall from the edge of the highway above. A road. There is a streetlight and there is rocks. Lots of rocks. The water becomes louder and I hear her.

"Down here Meme"....

"I'm stuck"…..

"It's so dark"…..

"It's so wet"….

"It's so cold"…..

I plop down on the vines, trees and dirt by the edge of the drop off and I put my head in my hands. "Why"????

I will never be able to get to her….

I'm pissed and He knows it. He knew it before I even got here. He knows all and sometimes I lose heart and He feels that. He knows this journey has been hard. He loves me so much. He knows I love Him so much.

After a good twenty minute cry. I finish explaining to Felicia…..

"Not yet sweetie"…..

He says "not yet".

"I must finish your project". "I must finish Ayla Faith's Learning Center".

"He loves you and He loves your mommie".

"Cora and I will concentrate on the learning center until we get further instructions".

"Meme will write your story, honey".

"I will do my best, that's all He asks".

"Please be patient and wait". "I love you to infinity and beyond"………….

The walk back to the car was hard and emotional I try my best to keep it together and He knows my heart is broken. He's done it before….

He knows I will survive….

He knows I am strong….

I am my mother's daughter!!!!!

Prelude to a Kiss

I thought I was done with Love Letters in the Sand-Ayla's Faith and He says "no".....

"Not Yet".….. Again just like Miracles Among Chaos my first book.….

I hear Him and I listen like a good girl!!!!

Blue Angels

He tells me "one more chapter Bella". My Col. Donald J. Strout. My morning dove who greets me in the morning and helps me end my days. A beautiful man indeed. A connection for me that not many will understand. A love from days gone by......

A past life time.....

That is another book and another love story for that is beautiful and pure and filled with God's true love.

God asks me to introduce some of the blue angels that have helped touch my life and to help me this lifetime to help spread God's love and His lessons within each blessing......

Top to bottom and none more important than God himself.....

Mother Mary

Mother Theresa

Princess Diana

Cherice Chase

Maya Angelo

Eleanor- Sam's mom

Eleanor-Cora's Grandmother

Eleanor-a- Jim's mother/grandmother figure

Grammie Stone, Grammie Helen, Grammie Cowing, Aunt Ede, Aunt Aggie, Aunt Mildred, Aunt Roberta.......

Rose- My music angel-personal.....

MJ, Whitney, Robin W., J-Lo's angel connections, Cameron D's angel connections, Rick Nelson, Elvis is in the building, Johnny's long black train is coming down the tracks—so many coming through I love them all and He says no more--- music angels and movie angel connections.........

OUR FATHER'S love is always present........

My father-Daddy-Andrew Allen Carter, Sr. I love you Daddy!

St. Germain- My Master Teacher

Sensei- My holistic healer connection

Melchezedeck- My Spiritual Law of Attraction High angel

St. Michael, St. Raphael, St. Uriel, St. Ariel..........

St. Lucifer

St. John

Moses....

Jonah, Noah...

St. Francis Assisi

Cleopatra

Romeo and Juliette

St. Paul (numbers too many)

All of my earth angels which are so many to list just like those who have passed from so long ago...

They, like He.....

Live within Me.....

Guess Who's back, guess who's back, guess who's back!!!! He shares with me this song to tell you all He never went anywhere!!!!!

Believe it or leave it.....

Pick it up and BE AMAZED....................................

I thank everyone I may have forgotten. God's love is so great my sacred heart beats new every single day for Him and all of his lost souls!!!!!

Bella Louise Allen

Proving Our Love

June 28, 2016

He asks me to prove Him and He will prove me. I do not hesitate with this love letter for Him. I love unconditionally and He shows me what true love is. The love between a mother and the love between a father.

I am in love with God. Our Father and creator of all that IS. He tries for so long to let me know I am LOVE….

I cannot believe or conceive it…..

I fear it and I hold my breath….

I am forty-nine years old and have truly never had a toe curling, love exploding, fireworks, in your face orgasm…..

Part of this journey is a gift for myself. I yet again am feeling let down by my Father. Not my Dad….. My MAKER!!!

On this journey with all of it I am given choices and He tells me I have free will. To do good and to do bad…..

This is where we draw the line in life….

The good between evil…..

Choosing to love ourselves over others.

This case is just that. This book is just that. I am just that.

I am a mother and I choose Little Miss Felicia's happiness over my own and He knew before I was born. He knew it when I chose to come back after my near death experience four years ago.

He loves us that much. He loves us enough to let us make choices for ourselves and this whole project. This whole book is a wakeup call for all of our bad choices.

Some of us have made better choices than others. Some of us have opened our eyes to God's love and there are more today than ever who are crushing the love of their OWN FATHER….

God is sick and He has lost HIS faith in us.

He loves us, but has lost HIS own faith. A gift he has given to each one of us and we squander it away like it is nothing.

A piece of garbage and it smells like rotten meat. Our children are paying the price and they are dying faster every day.

We take care of nothing that He gives us. The ocean is full of garbage. The streams are still over flowing with junk. The sides of the roads are disgusting. How can we look each other in the eyes knowing that God has a broken heart today and Mother Mary weeps tears and her body is literally wracked with pain from the children she has to console.

They are so many. They are so lost without the love of their loved ones.

My lesson for myself is that I still after all the love that I feel for my CREATOR....

MY FATHER-GOD

MY SON JESUS----Yes, my son Jesus....

Proven to me by His love through this journey.....

A past life time.

The man.

GOD

Reveals to me I am an incarnate many lifetimes ago. From the womb I bare His witness....

I sacrifice my own lamb.....

My own SON...

Jesus Christ......................

HE SAYS BELIEVE IT OR LEAVE IT!

In meditation He asks me to show him again how much I love Him. He asks me to show it through teaching myself tantric pleasures.....

A sin outlined in the Bible...

Yet He tells us in the Bible to love Him over no one.

We are each a piece of HIM from His own loin cloth we are cut.

I now know Mary's pain and I still choose my love for God. Above all else.

He gives me a choice I can either love Him and myself AND He will let me bring her home.

I have never met Little Miss Felicia but I love her with all of my heart as if I gave birth to her and I know my children and my love for them.

I would choose them over my own dead body.....

I would sacrifice it all for my children and I know in my heart there are so many more women out there that would give their very own life to have their child back in their lonely, lonely arms once again!!!

A never ending love story told by a woman who loves too much for everyone else and who will go to the ends of the earth for the love of her FATHER AND CHILD!!!

Working With The Universe

As Felicia's case comes to an end and we find her body. God's love will be restored to those who are willing to open their eyes, their hearts and their minds.

I work with God's creatures. Inside and out to learn His love is true in lives in everything that breath's and exists because of His grace and glory.

It only exists because He makes it so. Use it wisely and LOVE AND HAVE FAITH.

My animal kingdom is huge and they even reach across the ocean. I will only share with you these last two. They keep coming to me over and over through communication with this case and with learning my signs and symbols to bring our first baby home from the other side....

I carry a pocket guide to help me learn and to find His wonders in the animal world. My SPIRIT GUIDES are with my daily every day since October 29, 2015.

The ELEPHANT- Large and strong and to me I always associate the elephant with Dumbo....

A great love between a mother and her baby. A gift to the police from Little Miss Felicia from the other side.

"Ask and you shall receive".

"Seek and you shall find".

These words the love of my life reminds me of as we find the love He reminds me of over and over again from the beginning of this lifetime. Me at the age of three.

In the spirit world the meaning for the elephant is: Make it a point to be of service in some way to the young, elderly, or those less fortunate than yourself.

Do not let anything stand in the way of attaining this goal that is so integral to your purpose.

You have the determination and persistence required to overcome the current challenges that you're faced with.

Trust your senses, and if something in your life "smells" bad, take the necessary actions to do away with it.

Remain loyal to those closet to you in spite of anyone questioning your integrity.

It is a good time to renew your connectedness to the divine.

THE FALCON- A vivid dream in the early days of communication…..
He comes to an illuminated window…..
He waits while I learn and then He flies….
He waits again…
Patient and loving…..
He is my love and my light God/Jesus all in one.

The book says before making a decision, step back from it and consider it from a broader perspective.

There is an opportunity before you; however, be patient and trust your instincts to know when your time is right to act on it.

Pay closer attention to the natural rhythms of your body and of your surroundings, and see what this can teach you.

Whatever choice you make at this time, once you have made it, commit to it fully and take the plunge.

KITE- Take off your mask and let the world know who you really are.

Trust that none of what you have to deal with in the next few days will be a crisis, so do your best to remain calm and centered no matter what.

A few times a day take several slow breaths, deep breath and count to ten as you exhale. This clears your mind and helps you to make decisions that are divinely guided and centers and grounds you to be the best you, you can be.

FALLEN ANGEL ORACLE CARDS- Discover the art and wisdom of prediction by- Nigel Suckling

These cards are a new deck that I was guided to buy to help in my desperation for His truth…

These cards are a gift from God as is everything He creates. It is only the intention put to them that creates good or evil!!!

The first card drawn as Felicia's case comes to an end is beautiful.

A Large stone cross with etched crosses within the cross.

The word- GAAP (tap) Change and development

Elements- Air

Planet-Mercury

Message- Unless opposed by Bileth (20) this card bodes well. Act while your enemies are distracted.

Gaap is a powerful angel, almost the equal of Bileth (20) and a rival to him. According to legend, the gap was once found (by the magical spells of either Solomon or Noah's son, Shem) to serve Bileth in the composing of a book on mathematics, and has represented it ever since. So, when paired together Bileth and Gaap represent strife and discord. Alone Gaap, can stir either love or loyalty. He can steal the strength of enemies and afflict them with lethargy.

Card # 2

ZAGAN- Transformation

Element- fire

Planet- Sun

Zagan's totem beast is the bull, which links him to morax (15) and the apostle; Luke. Zagan was a patron of the old alchemists, possessing as he does the secrets of transmuting one material into another- base metal into gold, water into wine, blood into wine and vice versa, Some legends say it was Zagan who helped Jesus perform his miracle at the wedding in Cana and inspired the similar miracle at the last supper. Zagan is even able to make fools wise.

Card #3

BARBABTOS- Spirit of Nature

Element-air

Planet- Venus

Barbados can appear in dreams and visions as a beautiful archer on horseback in a forest, surrounded by four angels who are playing a fanfare of trumpets. She is a nature spirit who understands speech of all living creatures- birds, beasts, and even trees and plants. She favors those who are kind to the natural world. She is also the patroness of treasure hunters, knowing where ancient gold and jewels are buried in the wild, no matter what spells of concealment have been woven around them.

WISDOM OF THE HIDDEN REALMS- Oracle cards by Colette Baron-Reid

Moses comes to stand by me as I write these passage. He stands with his staff and smiles and the wrinkles of weariness are evident on his face. His eyes are cloudy and gray and he places his hand on my right shoulder.

I feel ease come to my heart and I get a thumbs up. He leaves as fast as he comes. A white feather floats to my lap and I cry. God sent me a kiss from Heaven by Moses appearance. Everything that has come to me is blessed and approved.

I draw the cards....

Card #1 is for the past-present-future.... Pay attention please!!!

THE WORD LORD- Communication, praise, dishonesty- #43

The Word Lord rules communication of all kinds and lets you know that positive interactions can be expected when he arrives as your Ally. He only speaks with positive words and praises all he sees. He reminds you of the laws of Abundance and Praise. When you bless the world, it blesses you back. When you say affirming, supportive words, they carry any energy that returns you in physical form. Remember that each one has power and will resonate into the universe, seeking its reflection in manifest form.

Your body responds to praise, as does everything in the world around you. Praise it for its inherent health and beauty. Applause yourself for everything you do, as even the tiniest accomplishments are important. Praise your bill: give thanks for the services you enjoy, and watch the ability to pay them increase as you align with Spirit's increasing power.

This is also a time to remember the powerful practice of affirmations. Write them down and speak them aloud as a spiritual exercise. Say it is so- and it will be. It's a very auspicious sign when the Word Lord chooses to be your Ally.

Challenger- When the Word Lord appears as your challenger, he gently warns of untruths, denial, and unsupportive thoughts and words in any area of your life. If you've been dishonest in any way, it's time to make amends. Change your tune; otherwise, your impact on the world will not be as effective as you would like. Even if you were to be successful as an immediate result, there would be a price to pay later.

If others are being unsupportive toward you, know that it's them, not you,. Don't take this world personally. Remember that you don't have to engage others when they project their own fears and negativity onto you.

Another message here is about how you speak about yourself. Do you say self-deprecating words? Do you minimize yourself so as not to intimidate others? Do you refer to yourself as less than beautiful? Time to change those unconscious statements now! It's not difficult to change things, as we are always given a choice to make new decisions. As long as you remain positive and supportive, the rest will quickly melt away

Until all you perceive is the highest good for all. All you need is a desire to change and be positive and the Word Lord will help you win the game of life!

Card # 2

THE ALTAR PRIESTESS- Preparation, Prayer, Sacred Ritual- 39

The stage is set and the world is waiting for you to take your place in sacred meditation and prayer. As your Ally, the Altar Priestess brings the ritual of reverent interaction with the mundane world. You're being required now to see everything sacred, all of life as a meditation, and every action as a prayer of devotion. When you're able to perceive the world in this way, your question will lead you to the appropriate answer.

If all is sacred, how can anything be wrong? Ask how you can shift your consciousness to see your circumstances through the eyes of the Divine and you will realize how perfect and sacred everything is right now.

Challenger- Are you degrading yourself in any way or lessening the importance of your impact in your world? Have you allowed someone to dishonor you? Have you failed to stand up for your beliefs in order to get something you want? The Altar Priestess warns that continuing on this path cold bring you trouble, as you may be aligning yourself with lower ideas as your companions.

Another message she brings you is this: never sell yourself short when it comes to your intuition. You're always led to the highest ground when you follow your inner guidance.

An important responsibility is brought to you when the Altar Priestess comes as your Challenger. You're being required to be a spiritual warrior and to have courage. Be ready, as you're being chosen to be the embodiment of the Sacred in the world. In essence, you're challenged to be the best you that you can be out there. You can do it, and Spirit is counting on it.

Card #3

THE PHEONIX- Resurrection, surrender to change- 29 (29 Violette)

The Phoenix appears as your Ally to celebrate your journey and to ensure your ultimate success. This is true even if it appears that you've just passed through a metaphorical experience of death or are currently enduring a perception of failure in your life.

Death and rebirth are related when you enter the realm of the Phoenix. Seen in this light, nothing truly dies, but rather changes from one ending directly into new beginnings. The Phoenix is constantly reinventing itself and rises up whole and new and even more powerful with every death it experiences. This could signal an end of a relationship-or of a dynamic within one-or an end of a job, a project, or even a life.

Perhaps no failure is involved, but it's time for a complete overhaul of your circumstances. You may be tired of what you're doing, or you may know intuitively that it's time to move on and try something new. Whatever the case, a death of the old and a celebration of new life are called for! Whatever you do now will indeed be a successful endeavor, for a rebirth is imminent!

Challenger- When the Phoenix challenges you, it's really just a gentle reminder to let go and let what doesn't work fall away. Maybe you're not allowing things to change because you're more comfortable with the familiar, even if you know that it's not the best you could create yourself.

Fear of change is a crippling experience, as it works against nature itself. The task at hand is to allow for an ending, as it's timely and right that you do so for the highest good of all. In surrendering to the fundamental purposeful change, you will most definitely find yourself in better circumstances. The action needed is allowing. A rebirth assured.

Georgia Peaches

As I learn more of His love I am amazed at all of the gifts He has placed in my life this time around and where they are all coming from.

He hands me the state Georgia over and over the past few months. He finally puts the two together. I visit my new grandbaby today. What a precious girl. So smart and she can't even walk yet. I see and He told me yesterday just part of her story and He asks me to see her. My special Georgia Peach. Why Georgia…..

George Washington and the Cherry tree. I get the name George in a message at the spiritualist church. A church I seek out answers for my new gifts.

I keep receiving the word my four father's and band of brothers. This piece comes together and so many seem to be falling into place and I can't keep up.

He shakes His hand and teases with me daily now. A God that is so alive He brings out pieces of me that I could never imagine. The love between us is so pure and strong I catch my breath and try to keep hold of my senses.

I keep seeing a special angel throughout the day. He is dressed in red. It is a long red robe and the robe is tied with a gold sache. I see Him standing in the fields everywhere today. He Is St. John Paul II….

Believe it or leave it He tells me again. I keep mental note of all the wonderful words, feelings, senses, sights and smells He shares with me on this journey. I hope to be able to write it all down but, He says I am good. Stop trying so hard.

The man in red goes with me to see my Granddaughter. What a wonderful loving man. He guides me to wash my hands first. He shows me an angel such as this deserves to be cleansed by God's gifts on earth for she is an angel pure as the mourning dove. He wants her to be baptized. Not for her sins but for the sins of those who still have not paid for her death.

Wow! I didn't see that one coming......

He knows who did it and I hope not to reveal it until He is ready for that. This journey is amazing and I ask again why me. He looks at me with His loving eyes and still it hasn't all sunk in.

He reminds me throughout my visit with my first granddaughter. I hold Princess Diana's first incarnate and I am Mother Mary and He loves me for all of my own sacrifices. That is why He continues to love me......

I visit with Hayley today and we talk in length about her hopes and dreams and she shares her trials that are keeping her from sleeping and wondering again where her own God has gone. He escaped her when she was seven years old and states "She was ripped from His arms". She struggles daily with her own faith and belief in her purpose in this world.

Hayley, to was diagnosed with Bi-Polar at a young age. Judged for her gifts and misunderstood. She has the same signs I have only she hides from them. I believe with God's grace and St. John's visit with us today she now sees HIS light just a little brighter.

After an emotional visit and much spirit coming through for both of us she feels better and supported in her journey and I let her know I am so grateful to her for being a rock for my lost son. I thank her for giving birth to her own miracle baby a princess sent back for another chance to share her beauty and grace. Praise be to God He is risen!!!

The Lady in the lake

Another past life connection is handed to me and I am amazed. He shares with me my own meditation in the tub. The day I pulled a child from the waters. Dead and dark hair across her face. Earth shattering to see yet He helps me be strong and I love Him for that.

Connections between the two are shown to me by St. John Paul II. As we converse I sit back and observe Hayley and the baby and watch her angels speak and work through her actions.

Another Cinderella story in the making I'm sure. God shared with me a few days back 7 years of tribulation are over for me and my family. We are being blessed in all areas and He thanks me for all of my own faith and love in Him.

Hayley shares with me a connection with this information that was coming in. A man old and he has lots of hair. I immediately get Merlin. Then the flood gates open.

My daughter Ann Marie was Merlin. A sorcerer from days gone by. She loves magic she loves fantasy she is a miracle girl who bore the Miracle baby. My hero. This story truly is deeper than dead.

I watch her teach him with her own magical kingdom of angels and she doesn't even believe in God, Mother Mary or Jesus......

She will be my toughest egg to crack. My own closest link to this world and she suffered so much the day she witnessed my second break down. I can never take it away. I can only say I am sorry for being so weak.

I have tried so hard for so long and I still apologize to all that I love for the person I feel I fail to be. A mother who would end her own life for all of her love for those around her.

St. John Paul II shares with me as I share a great revelation of its own with Hayley and my granddaughter another miracle in my life this lifetime.

Another love story

My first born child, this lifetime…..

A baby girl born to my God Mother, Joyce. A wonderful love story all of her own. She has unending faith in God and Prays the Rosary faithfully. Yet she doesn't take time to listen to any of her prayers being sent up. She has lived the life of a whirlwind and God asks her to sit still. Listen and hear His heart, it beats with yours.

My first Crystal child….

Metaphorically speaking

My moon baby I called her and so did her dad. Crystal such a wonderfully faithful young mother. Loses her only daughter in a tragic accident and almost lost her son the same day. Another Cinderella story to be written.

A tragedy that struck me hard for I have love that moon baby with all of my heart since her mother first entrusted her in my care. I did the only thing I could think of when she was suffering so much pain and loss. I started a fund raising project to help ease the burden financially. For too many months they sat in the hospital waiting for a miracle to happen after the loss of Theresa. They waited for Caden to waken from his own tragic story.

Why do I feel sympathy for others? Why do I cry tears of blue? Why do I see so much pain? I have lived this pain life time after life time?

I am Mother Mary. I witnessed my own son sacrificed at the cross so long ago. I survived that tragedy and I am strong because He lives within me now and forever until the end of time.

I am reminded of my dreamtime. A few nights back I awaken at 4:44 and I ask for sanctuary. A reprieve from all of this agony. God I beseech you for help with all of this. I am your daughter, Bella. I am only one girl standing before you asking for you to show me compassion and love and I need a break!!!!

The Fire With in My Soul

He takes me back to the beginning. I sit naked as He has guided me to. To conceive just how wonderful life should be. A life of simplicity and shame free. He tells me all He wishes me to know. This book will not be the last. It wasn't the first. But it will knock your socks off.

Love Letters in the Sand- Ayla's Faith is just that. A beautiful tale. A tale of His love for the world and all that is in it. He created man and so man wouldn't be lonely he created woman. He and I, Seth and I are in HIS likeness. Pure of soul yet we are not sin free.

He has had a plan from the beginning and we HIS people have failed. He is back and He cries and mourns daily with Mother Mary. Me. Bella.

As I walk that lonely dirt road one more time He shows me the fire and the moon. He is the sun and I am His moon beam. He is the masculine part of me. I am the feminine part of HIM.

He created Adam. In a suit of armor to be His king then. He created Eve to be His Queen then.

Johnny's apple seed.....

I failed His commandment first. I will pay for that sin until the end of all time. I still suffer today and He knows it. He tries to help me reconnect with myself these last few months as He teaches me all of my worth.

God shares with me so many beautiful things in this one book. A Romeo and Juliette story relived for sure.

Little Miss Felicia and so many others have become victim to the sin of the flesh. It is evident wherever you go.

In that sin stems so much more. Greed, lust, Hate, resentment, fear, loathing, fornication and killing. It is out of control and His fire is nearly out. He can no longer sustain this world without some HOPE, FAITH AND ABOVE ALL LOVE.

In Love Letters in the Sand-Ayla's Faith it shows so much love and so much loss. God wonders where He went wrong.....

What did He do to make everyone lose FAITH?

Reconnecting with self is the hardest thing to do. Learning to love oneself is not an easy job. It can be a beautiful thing as will be portrayed in another book.

The Fire in the soul is a beautifully written book on the very core of the issue underlying in so many child abuse cases, lost marriages and even the underlying issues in the churches.

God made us man and woman for a reason. To love. Those of us who chose to stand alone made some pretty horrible choices.

The flesh is very tender and it has receptors and feelings that run deeper than the surface. Love runs back to the core of God.

Back to the core of Adam and Eve.

You cannot quench this thirst.

This fire in the soul is a love for God. By hiding your love. You cannot kill your thirst for God by laying down. You cannot kill your thirst for God by ignoring it. You cannot kill your lust for God by running away from it.

So many people struggle with fighting this fire that we have ended up in a destitute world full of depraved. Deprived. Blood thirsty killers.

It must be quenched.

This fire in the soul.

Search out this Fire and put it out for if you don't the lights will go out on the world forever.

Sickness and hopelessness are just scratching the surface.

Misdiagnosis of so many illnesses are running rampant.

We are putting innocent children away in institutes, in graves and sending them out into the world unarmed without His grace and love.

We must readjust our thinking and go back to the beginning of time before it is too late.

The news is filled with the plagues of days gone by and we just sit on our hands and watch it happen. Wondering why!

We empaths, we holistic healers who have been burned at the stake for centuries have watched and vomited our insides out just like God is doing now.

Mother Mary-Me......

I still pay the price for my first sins….

Eve and Mary. God's first true love's…..

Judged and scorned for HIS love.

God asks to pray the rosary…..

Respect your mother…..

Give her what is owed….

God asks you to bend down on your knees and pray for forgiveness and hold your children tight…..

They are the world and their future will not exist unless you do.

The end….
I hope not!!

Printed in the United States
By Bookmasters